Are you interested

a course management system that would

save you time & effort?

If the answer is *yes*, **CourseCompass is for you.**

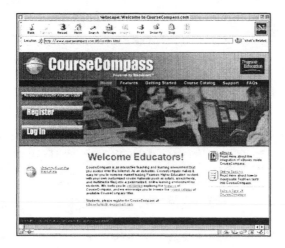

CourseCompass is an online course management system
designed to help you manage all the aspects of your course –
communication, information distribution, testing and grading.

Let it help you:

- **Communicate directly with your students** via email, discussion
boards, and announcement pages.

- **Post documents for your course,** eliminating the need for course
packs or handouts.

- **Administer online tests,** with automatic grading and analysis.

- **Provide your students with 24/7 access** to key course information,
such as syllabus, assignments, and additional resources – as well as
check his/her grade instantly.

Demo CourseCompass today! www.coursecompass.com

Open-Book Testing: Why It Makes Sense

By Kay Burke, Ph.D.

Educators who allow students to take open-book tests are not teaching *for the test*; they are teaching *for understanding*. Most students agree that open-book tests are more challenging than traditional objective tests because they require high-order thinking skills rather than recall skills.

The greatest benefit from open-book testing may be that it encourages the type of thinking that will benefit students in the real world.

- Open-book tests focus on students learning important concepts rather than memorizing facts.

- They encourage students to utilize the lifelong learning skill of "accessing information" rather than memorizing data. In most jobs, people do not have to memorize formulas or discrete bits of data; they have to know how to find the important information they need in order to solve problems and complete projects.

- Open-book tests encourage students to highlight the text and organize their notes so they can find the information they need.

- Open-book tests encourage students to **apply** the information they have learned and **transfer** it to new situations, rather than just repeat the facts.

Sources:

Burke, K.B. *The mindful school: How to assess authentic learning.* Arlington Heights, IL. Skylight Professional Development.

Stiggins, R.J. (1985, October). *Improving assessment where it means the most: In the classroom.* Educational Leadership, pp. 69-74.

Wiggins, G. (1989, April). *Creating tests worth taking.* Educational Leadership, pp. 121-127

Wiggins, G., & McTighe, J. (1989). *Understanding by design.* Alexandria, VA: Association for Supervision and Curriculum Development.

Instructor's Manual and Test Bank

for

Karger and Stoesz

American Social Welfare Policy
A Pluralist Approach

Fifth Edition

prepared by

Nancy Jane Otto
University of Houston

Boston   New York   San Francisco
Mexico City   Montreal   Toronto   London   Madrid   Munich   Paris
Hong Kong   Singapore   Tokyo   Cape Town   Sydney

ISBN 0-205-46419-X

Printed in the United States of America

10 9 8 7 6 5 4 3 2 1   09 08 07 06 05

Table of Contents

Introduction

Instructor's Manual

Test Bank

INTRODUCTION

Social policy courses are "standard fare" for MSW programs, and Karger & Stoez's *American Social Welfare Policy* is one of the most well-written and highly utilized texts in social work education. As an instructor using the 5th edition of their text, you obviously recognize that a strong foundation grounded in the understanding and integration of social policy into practice will likely determine a student's ability to transition from the classroom into a productive and meaningful career.

As a former student of one of the authors, I had the opportunity to develop this supplemental text with "framer's intent" in mind. A balanced, comprehensive, and sophisticated look at the changing face of American policy and economics, as well as an ability to openly discuss and debate key issues are integral ingredients for the learning process to occur. They are also components of this text that are second to none.

This breadth and depth of coverage and discussion, however, is not easily digested; American social welfare policy is often difficult to comprehend and always a complex and ever-changing issue. This instructor's manual, therefore, was designed to assist you in imparting to your classes how and why understanding social policy is important to becoming an effective professional social worker. Hopefully, you will find that this manual provides you with a springboard for classroom instruction and discussion.

This publication was designed to assist you in summarizing, choosing focal points, and incorporating pertinent discussion into class time for each chapter. Additionally, there is an emphasis on consistency in this manual – each chapter has key learning points, ten "Teaching Suggestions," five "Classroom Discussion" questions, a "Spotlight Box" and a test bank consisting of 15 multiple choice, 15 essay, and 10 true/false questions. These summaries and questions are not intended to serve as an exhaustive resource, but rather as a catalyst for your own talents and interests to come to life in a cooperative, holistic, and complete learning environment.

Congratulations on choosing *American Social Welfare Policy* as the text of choice for your social policy course. You have chosen well and your students will no doubt benefit from your use of the text and supplementary materials concurrently. Comments and suggestions for future editions of this instructor's manual are always welcome and appreciated. Best of luck in your teaching endeavors and thank you for your commitment to the promulgation of social work education.

Nancy Jane Otto
University of Houston, Graduate School of Social Work

Chapter 1

Social Policy and the American Welfare State

Chapter Overview

In chapter one, the authors provide a broad overview of our nation's response to social problems. The manner in which our welfare state responds to these social problems is influenced by the ideology of both conservatives and liberals and as varied as the responses are, so too are the definitions of social welfare policy. The definition offered by William Epstein is insightful: policy is "social action sanctioned by society," a collective response to particular problems. This chapter examines the way in which political ideology and economics influence the policies that shape the American welfare state.

Learning Objectives

1. American social welfare is evolving. After 70 years of experimenting with the welfare state, a discernable shift to conservatism is occurring.

2. Liberals frequently see such programs as a means of helping the disadvantaged. Conservatives frequently question public sector approaches and argue for private solutions.

3. The pluralistic mix of private and public services is a primary feature of American social welfare, and the American social welfare system is in contrast with the systems in most other major nations.

4. Social welfare is big business, as evidenced by scope of services and programs and by the extent to which for-profit firms become increasingly involved in the provision of health and human services.

5. The coexistence of voluntary, governmental, and corporate sectors create challenges for clients, direct service workers, and administrators.

6. Definitions of social welfare policy abound. Titmuss sees policy and services as "a series of collective interventions…" which redistribute income.

7. Social welfare policy develops in response to social problems and determines the availability of income, food, health care, housing, and personal social services.

8. The political economy in the US is one of democratic capitalism, meaning that a representative form of government coexists with a market economy.

9. Economics forms the backbone of the political system and Keynesian, Free Market, and Socialist economies are discussed in regard to the influence on American political economy.

Teaching Suggestions and Exercises for Student Learning

1. Ask students to brainstorm reasons this course may be required. Discuss their answers. Some of the answers may sound like application essays. If no student mentions CSWE or accreditation, refer to CSWE's standards as one reason such courses are required, and ask why CSWE requires such curriculum content. If no student identifies the need for social workers to be aware of the broad range of social problems and social programs in the US, be sure to include this.

2. Brainstorm social problems in the US. This can usually be accomplished in 5-7 minutes if the instructor refrains from commenting and simply lists the problems. From here, there are many options. Students could be asked to prioritize problems. They could identify problems such as poverty or substance abuse that are connected to many other problems. They could be prepared to recognize these problems and relevant social programs as they read the text.

3. Ask students to be thinking about who makes social policy and how is it made? This may be part of the curriculum content in other policy courses at the school. If not, it is useful to explore these areas and to go beyond the "three branches of government." The text's pluralism framework is particularly relevant.

4. The instructor could also diagram two policy continua, as shown below. This can be used as a discussion exercise or simply a reminder that all four factors are at work in many policy-making endeavors, even though most social policy is incremental. It should be noted on the horizontal continuum that most enacted social welfare policies in recent years have been incremental; the Social Security Act of 1935 is an example of more comprehensive legislation. On the vertical continuum, one can usually find both forces at work; which is more influential is the subject of never-ending debate.

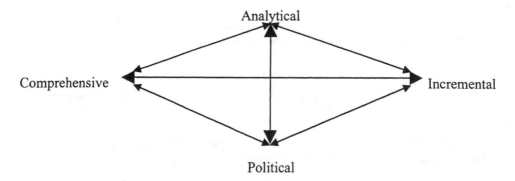

5. The authors' discussion of the economic and political forces that influence social welfare is extensive. This section includes historical and contemporary issues. Some students may not see the distinction between liberals and neoliberals or conservatives and neoconservatives. It is useful to start with the broader distinctions between liberal and conservative philosophies and approaches. Then one can expand and make sure that students understand the wide variety of policy forces and the extent to which there are think tanks and interest groups advocating different approaches to government and social policy.

6. Social policy courses can be enhanced by incorporating contemporary events in discussing many of the issues in this chapter. For example, discuss Greens Party influence on the most recent presidential elections.

7. Many social workers have argued that the US is a "reluctant welfare state." Ask students how they see this. Why is the US called a "reluctant welfare state?" Ask students to begin thinking about how does the US social welfare system compares with systems in Western Europe and/or systems in developing nations.

8. Obtain a copy of Keynes's book, *The General Theory of Employment, Interest and Money*. Have students identify basic components of Keynesian Economics in the text.

9. Take each of the political persuasions discussed in Chapter 1 and have students collaborate on finding a contemporary or historical leader who indicates each political persuasion best.

10. Have students discuss their opinion regarding the "proper" role of the federal government in Social Welfare.

Classroom Discussion Questions

1. The notion of political-economy reminds us that the United States is a Democracy with a free enterprise, capitalist economy. How do these conflict? What kinds of compromises are necessary? What is a "Mixed Welfare Economy?" Okun's (1975) Equality and Efficiency: The Big Tradeoff, though dated, is a classic explication.

2. Can human service corporations care for the poor and multiproblem clients while continuing to generate profits? What ethical issues are involved?

3. With what political persuasion do you most closely identify? If none exactly, what tenets of each?

4. Discuss the following quote from John Judis and Michael Lind, "Ultimately, American economic policy must meet a single test: Does it, in the long run, tend to raise or depress the incomes of most Americans." Using this litmus test, what social welfare policies pass, which fail?

5. Albert Einstein said, "We cannot solve the problems of today with the same level of thinking that created them." Discuss this concept in relation to American social welfare policy.

Spotlight Box

The Hoover Institution, based at Stanford University, helped to shape the early conservative position on welfare. Visit their website at http://www-hoover.stanford.edu/ and determine the issues they are currently discussing that may have the biggest impact on social welfare policy, positively or negatively.

Chapter 2 — Social Welfare Policy Research: A Framework for Policy Analysis

Chapter Overview

This chapter provides a concise overview of policy research and proposes one model for policy analysis. The authors emphasize that a desire to remedy social problems is the first step leading to policy proposals, and ultimately policy change. Political, economic, and administrative feasibility are major considerations for analysts of these proposals. Primary research resources are discussed with a special section devoted to internet research, ethical guidelines surrounding this research, and several of the major think tanks and advocacy organizations that may provide an initial springboard for policy analysis.

Learning Objectives

1. A policy framework is a systematic and structural means by which to examine the congruence of a policy with the mission and goals of the social welfare state.

2. Policy frameworks can:
   a. Help determine if a policy is consistent with social welfare values and/or historical precedents
   b. Compare existing and competing policies
   c. Determine the roles of a social worker on a micro/macro level
   d. Assist in best practices for environmental scanning

3. Well-designed policy frameworks vary in their design and purpose. There are typically eight key elements which emphasize the systematic, contextual, and analytical nature of successful and well-developed policy frameworks that include:
   a. Systematic analysis
   b. Concise contextual framework by which to judge the policy options
   c. Rational methods of inquiry and analysis
   d. Explicit analytical method, typically represented by high repeatability
   e. Utilitarian goals – policies that create the greatest good for the most people
   f. Consideration to unintended results of a policy
   g. Examination of alternative paradigms through which to solve the same problem
   h. Consideration of long and short term impacts of the policy

4. Historically, one can identify many examples of well-intentioned policies with less-than-satisfactory results. A current example is the policy of drug interdiction and enforcement.

5. There is no single analytic paradigm for policy analysis. However, the model incorporates many of the usual and customary approaches, analytic criteria, resources, and ideas relevant to the social work profession. Most analytic paradigms incorporate: adequacy, equity, economy, effectiveness, efficiency, and political and administrative feasibility.

6. In analyzing a policy's viability, it is essential to look at its political, economic, and administrative feasibility.

7. There are some primary sources of information relative to Congressional policy. In addition to government examples, the authors cover major think tanks, advocacy organizations and professional associations. *The Encyclopedia of Associations* is a useful resource for developing an expanded list of sources.

8. While online research is a burgeoning facet of policy analysis, one must be cognizant of ethical issues involving informed consent and confidentiality of research participants.

Teaching Suggestions and Exercises for Student Learning

1. Break the class into small learning groups for the duration of the semester. Assign each group a social welfare policy currently being considered at the state or federal level. Applying the authors' four-pronged model for policy analysis, have each learning group identify strengths and potential problem areas for their policy's implementation.

2. Have the class come up with several examples of what the text refers to as "social problems driving social policies."

3. Now, encourage learners to identify examples of social policies that, in the end, perpetuated the social problem.

4. Encourage students to select a current bill concerning social welfare policy and over the course of the semester, track legislative debate surrounding the economic, administrative, and political efficiency of the proposed bill. This exercise is especially exciting and useful if your state's legislature is in session.

5. Have the small learning groups determine a social problem that is of particular interest to them, identifying the significance of the problem and its macro-level effects. Instruct groups to develop a social welfare policy to combat the problem with special consideration given to the administration and financing of this policy. Stage a classroom debate wherein students analyze each policy for the fulfillment of its objectives. Additionally, have another small learning group come up with an alternative plan of action to combat this social ill.

6. Contact your local United Way and arrange to have their policy analyst perform a guest lecture during one of your classes.

7. Participate in a "Student Lobby Day" with your municipal or state representatives. Have the class research a social issue affecting your area and devise recommendations that students may make to their representatives at this "Lobby Day."

8. Obtain a *Green Book* of the House Committee on Ways and Means from your local or university library. Have the class identify populations or social welfare issues not currently being addressed. Encourage the class to critically identify reasons why this population or issue has remained unsolved.

9. Contact a think-tank organization in your area. Arrange for one of their representatives to perform a guest lecture.

10. Obtain a copy of your Institutional Research Board's (IRB) policies and guidelines for research. Determine as a class how internet research is governed by this entity.

Classroom Discussion Questions

1. How can a social work practitioner utilize effective policy analysis on a micro level? Macro level?

2. Social workers are trained to work within the system to affect positive change for underserved populations. How can policy analysis, both effective and errant, hinder this process?

3. What will be the most challenging aspect for you personally in conducting policy analysis and operationally applying those findings to your future organization?

4. What suggestions can you make to improve the text's model for developing an effective policy analysis framework.

5. What current programs, locally and federally, would benefit from an effective policy analysis framework?

Spotlight Box

The website http://www.onlinepolicy.org addresses the safety, security, and legitimacy of many online research models, as well as issues facing online researchers and students alike. Browse the website and invite class discussion regarding some of the issues the website presents.

Chapter **3**

Religion and
Social Welfare Policy

Chapter Overview

Chapter 3 is a new inclusion to the 5th edition of *American Social Welfare Policy*. The diversity and strength of our nation's religious entities are unequaled by other societies and its influence has a marked affect on social welfare policy. The historical significance of religion and its influence on these policies is addressed at great length, as are the implications of legislation, programs, and funding in contemporary society, as influenced by Judeo-Christian principles. The introduction of Bush's White House Office of Faith-Based and Community Initiatives has been a controversial issue, as has the left's secularization of government and the New Christian Right's response to this occurrence.

Learning Objectives

1. In 1601, the introduction of the English Poor Laws brought to light the Church's influence in government. For the most part, the Laws were administered through church parishes and by religious leaders.

2. The Protestant Work Ethic, evidenced in Colonial America, fueled the creation of a work-oriented society, and the ideology that "worthy" and "unworthy" poor existed began to strongly emerge.

3. The Second Great Awakening is pointed to as being a lasting influence on social welfare policy. The movement saw private organizations taking on more responsibility for societal ills, and women and ethnic minorities began to emerge as leaders and advocates for social services.

4. The rise of social work as a profession began in the late 1800's. Counter to social workers of today in theoretical charge, workers of this time period made subjective assessments of need based on impoverished families' contrition, work ethic, and religious values.

5. Charity Organization Societies first became evident in the 1870's, with rising popularity and growth in most major cities. Settlement houses, the best known being Hull House, were known for integrating workers and their areas, and are perhaps the first models of intensive, community-based management of services.

6. Free, religion-based radio programming, which began to emerge in the late 1920's, paved the way for the masses to be exposed to American religious life.

7. Beginning in 1940, the government began to more adamantly secularize, marked by Supreme Court cases and state laws prohibiting an intermarriage of "church and state."

8. Mainstream religions and their influence began to decline in the 50's and 60's.

9. As a response to secularization and mainstream religion's decline, movements such as the Christian Right emerged, which took a political and religious stance on social welfare policy.

10. Since George W. Bush's first term in office, faith-based methods for providing social services have increased, despite their controversial implications in regard to the First Amendment.

Teaching Suggestions and Exercises for Student Learning

1. The authors assert that American social welfare policy is largely based on influences of Christianity. Obtain a copy of the *Holy Bible* and cite references that confirm or deny this assertion.

2. Determine whether or not your school's reference library has access to the Elizabethan Poor Laws. Have the class look over and determine what laws may still have their influence on American social welfare policy.

3. Have your students do an informal survey of congregations and/or faith-based organizations that provide social services in your area. What various services are provided and under what circumstances? Is there a clear absence of any kind of social services offered by these groups?

4. Read Dean Keeley's *Why Conservative Churches are Growing*. Discuss how this 1950's book applies in our contemporary society.

5. Invite your students to go beyond the headlines and examine the realities of faith-based service delivery systems as they operate in the present-day practice community. Have them compare faith-based delivery systems with traditional, welfare, clinical, entrepreneur, and human service sector providers in terms of value-base, expertise, social mandates, and resources available to meet needs of marginalized populations.

6. Select a faith-based agency in the community (Catholic Social Services, Jewish Family Services would be examples). Set up an appointment to interview an administrator of that agency. Focus the interview on how that agency services a specific population in terms of staffing and budget. Inquire about laws and policies external to the agency that empower the agency to provide services to the population selected. Ask the administrator to provide you a copy of the agency's mission statement. Oftentimes mission statements provide insight to the values of an agency. Repeat this process with a non faith-based agency servicing the same population. Compare/contrast in terms of values, expertise of staff, social mandates, and resources. What did the students learn about contemporary faith-based agencies and what can they suggest about the future of faith-based initiatives?

7. Have students watch or listen to a religious broadcasting segment and critically analyze any messages that might be disseminated regarding religion's obligation to social services in the US.

8. Obtain a copy of NASW's Code of Ethics. Which components may be considered as influenced by religion?

9. Find recent commentary or news articles discussing the religious and anti-religious movements. How has each affected American social welfare policy?

10. Have students research the units of President Bush's Faith-Based and Community Initiatives in the Departments of Labor, Justice, Housing and Urban Development, Education, and Health and Human Services. How do their offerings vary among each unit?

Classroom Discussion Questions

1. Are faith-based organizations and their federal funding constitutional? Why or why not?

2. How has religion impacted social welfare policy and the practice of social work over the years?

3. Is the availability of funding likely to change the attitudes of religious organizations to social services?

4. Discuss how Title XX affects faith-based funding.

5. If you practice a particular religion, how does it view social welfare policy? Do you agree or disagree with this approach?

Spotlight Box

Jerry Falwell, noted as the founder of the Moral Majority, has inflamed both religious and non-religious persons with assertions regarding politics, homosexuality, prayer in schools, etc. Conversely, he has many "followers" who promulgate his message. View Rev. Falwell's website http://www.falwell.com and discuss among the class whether or not these messages are overt or hidden.

Chapter 4

Discrimination in American Society

Chapter Overview

This chapter examines racism and its effects from the perspectives of personality and cultural influences. Institutional discrimination against African Americans, Hispanics, Native Americans, Asian Americans, and women is discussed in terms of social, economic, and health indicators. Civil rights legislation and affirmative action initiatives are highlighted, as is the struggle for equal protections for people who are lesbian or gay. The effects of ageism and discrimination against persons with disabilities are contrasted with legislative efforts aimed to level the societal playing field.

Learning Objectives

1. In this chapter, discrimination is discussed in the economic, social, and political realms. The text links discrimination to poverty and the need for social reform and social programs.

2. Various reasons for discrimination are given, including psychological theories, cultural theories, and economic activity leading to discrimination. Racism is discussed as a type of discrimination.

3. The authors focus on discrimination against different populations, and provide statistics comparing each minority group with the current US majority, as well as offering information specific to each minority group. It is important to note that the text cites the US Census Bureau statistics indicating that whites will no longer be the majority in the United States by 2050.

4. An important facet of this chapter deals with changes in immigration practices and law since 9/11. According to the text, fewer immigrants and refugees are being allowed into the country's borders, with more stringent guidelines and rules governing their time in the United States.

5. The feminization of poverty is a reflection that the playing field in the United States is not equal and that sexism has been institutionalized in public policy.

6. Although nationwide polls and recent legislative action has show favor toward those in the homosexual lifestyle (estimated at between 1% and 10% of the United States population), statistics presented in the text paint a picture that suggests their fight is far from over. Despite health and economic gains made by senior citizens over the past three decades, a sizeable population (less than 12%) remains in poverty. Attention to the economic, social and emotional needs of seniors is oftentimes blunted by a United States culture pre-occupied with youthfulness, and ill-prepared to address the needs made prevalent by longer life-spans.

7. The Americans with Disabilities Act (1990) prohibits discrimination on the basis of disability in employment, state and local government activities, and in public accommodations and services. The courts will decide on questions of applicability and definition of disability.

8. There have been numerous attempts to eliminate discrimination and many legal proceedings that have established important legal precedents for ethnic minorities, women, the aged, homosexuals, and the disabled. Several of these attempts are featured in the chapter.

Teaching Suggestions and Exercises for Student Learning

1. Encourage the class to debate whether or not the term "middle class" is an appropriate classification. How do each of the students personally identify now in the social stratification system? Growing up?

2. Have students look up and research various legal remedies to combat discrimination (pages 97-101 of the text). Invite students to present to other members of the class regarding their findings.

3. Have a guest speaker from your area Women's Center or women's health care clinic guest lecture regarding the effects of sexism on violence, rape and women's health care.

4. Select an article from the *New York Times* dealing with a social policy issue. Discuss the article chosen in terms of this statement: Social problems are not distributed evenly throughout the general population – specific groups bear disproportionate burdens.

5. Discuss evidence that supports or does not support personality, cultural, moral, religious, and political influences in the development of prejudicial attitudes.

6. Discuss the concept of 'diswelfare'. Apply to populations students work with in practicum.

7. The U.S. has the most advanced medicine in the world. How do you account for the overall ranking (25th) in Infant Mortality Rates in Table 4.2? How do you account for the differences in U.S. rankings in that same table when broken down by white only, Native American, and black only?

8. Discuss the pros and cons of Native Americans establishing independent health, education, and welfare services as in the Indian Self-Determination Act of 1975.

9. Have students stage a debate to discuss how the term "marriage" should be defined. Ensure that the class is equally divided and encourage students to sit on the "side" that they personally disagree with … an exercise in mind expansion, tolerance, and critical thinking.

10. Using figures from the most recent US census, determine how many residents of your community are: minority, over 65 years, living at or below the poverty line. How do these numbers affect your community dynamics? Policies? Social work education? Opportunities for field practicum?

Classroom Discussion Questions

1. If the "minority" becomes the population majority, should they still be considered "minority" and receive benefits afforded historically oppressed populations?

2. Should the term "middle class" be more or less stringently defined? Why or why not?

3. The Immigration Act of 1990 favored highly skilled applicants gaining entry into the U.S. What criteria do you think the United States should use to make immigration decisions? Relate ethical reasoning to the criteria chosen.

4. From your experiences as a student in practicum agencies, do you see evidence of glass ceilings and sexist policies in those organizations? Discuss the office culture of the agency: is it supportive of fair working conditions?

5. Identify ramifications that longer life-spans will have for health, economic, and social policy. Discuss of how these policy measures will inform future practice directions.

Spotlight Box

In 1985, Rev. Jesse Jackson, Sr. established the Rainbow Coalition. His purpose in doing so is best stated in his own words, "The American Dream is one big tent of many cultures, races and religions. Under that tent, everybody is assured equal protection under the law, equal opportunity, equal access and a fair share. Our, struggle demands that we open closed doors, extend the tent and even the playing field." Since its inception, the Coalition has spoken out and advocated for many causes, particularly the end of racism and discrimination. On their website: www.rainbowpush.org, the Coalition discusses their foci:

- Jobs and Economic Empowerment
- Employee Rights and Livable Wages
- Educational Access
- Fair and Decent Housing
- Voter Registration and Civic Education
- Election Law Reform
- Fairness in the Media, Sports, and Criminal Justice System
- Political Empowerment
- Trade and Foreign Policy
- Affirmative Action and Equal Rights
- Gender Equality
- Environmental Justice

Chapter 5

Poverty in
America

Chapter Overview

This is one of the central chapters of the book. Social policy is a response to social problems and poverty is arguably one of our nation's most pervasive social problems. This chapter provides a thorough description of the nature and extent of poverty in the US and how it has changed over the past forty years. The distinction between absolute and relative poverty is important and many argue that the absolute poverty standard is too low for adequate subsistence. Thus, there are a number of "not poor" but "near poor" whose needs should be considered by policy makers. The broader issue of economic inequality is important as well in that US inequality is more extreme than inequality in most other developed nations.

Learning Objectives

1. Poverty in America is unique as compared and contrasted with poverty in developed and underdeveloped nations.

2. Poverty is both simple and complex. Students need to understand the simple facts as a starting point: who is poor, how many are poor, how does poverty vary by race, ethnicity, family status, family size, etc.

3. An understanding of absolute and relative poverty and the implications of these terms' usage is important. Much US policy is based on the needs of the relatively poor. For example, the current policy debate over senior citizen's need for help in paying for prescription drugs is focused more on the relatively than the absolutely poor because many of the absolutely poor can qualify for Medicaid. However, many relatively poor cannot qualify for Medicaid and cannot afford their prescriptions or supplemental medical insurance.

4. There are many theories of poverty: cultural, racial, family, radical, and many others. There are conservative and liberal ideological positions. The various ideologies discussed in the first chapter represent different ideas about how and why people are poor and what can be done to remedy their situations.

5. The radical perspective holds that poverty is caused by exploitation and by larger social and economic forces that perpetuate poverty. Many students and professional social workers subscribe to this position.

6. Table 5.1, Persons below the Poverty Line, is very important. Among the key points to stress:
   - Poverty varies by age, family status, and ethnicity.
   - Poverty has changed dramatically since 1959.
   - Between 1959 and 1969, poverty declined by nearly 50%.
   - The poverty rate for the aged declined sharply from 35% in 1959 to 10% in 2002.
   - The poverty rate for individuals in female-headed households has been persistently high, though marked decreases since 1959 are evident.
   - Poverty varies considerably among Blacks, Whites, and those of Hispanic origin.

7. Table 5.2, Changes in the Poverty Line Based on Income and Family Size, illustrates that the absolute poverty standard can be misleading. In 2003, an individual with a yearly income of $9,394 may not be considered "poor" but still may not be able to afford basic necessities.

8. The federal government's estimate of poverty raises many questions.

9. Rural poverty is greatly misunderstood.

10. The section on work and poverty merits special study. It illustrates the simplicity and complexity of poverty. The conventional wisdom holds that work helps to escape poverty. This is valid up to a point, but there are many low-wage jobs and many "working poor."

11. Table 5.4, The Value of the Minimum Wage, provides important information that students should fully understand. Note the trends from 1965-70.

12. Strategies to combat poverty, introduced in both the public and private sector, warrant inclusion in class discussion.

13. The section on America's fringe economy discusses ways in which a capitalist society exploits the needs of our nation's most impoverished individuals and families.

Teaching Suggestions and Exercises for Student Learning

1. If the class is comprised of more experienced students, many issues can be discussed as open-ended rhetorical questions or brainstorming issues. For example, from Table 5.1, Persons Below the Poverty Line:
   - Why did overall poverty decline more dramatically from 1959 to the early 1970's?
   - Did the major decline start in 1960 or later?
   - How and why has so much progress been made among the elderly? Have social programs been a factor?
   - After 1969, poverty among children began rising again—why?
   - In other developed countries, poverty in female-headed families is less serious. Why? What do these countries do differently? Are there any value issues at work in the US? What does this say about US priorities?
   - The overall poverty rate is dramatically lower for Whites. Why? Brainstorm a variety of explanations.

2. Using Table 5.2, Changes in the Poverty Line Based on Income and Family Size, add a dollar/subtract a dollar: are those who are poor necessarily worse off and those with incomes just above poverty better off? What other factors, such as where one lives, affect the poverty standard? How does this illustrate the simplicity and complexity of poverty?

3. Ask class members to write what they consider a "reasonable minimum" annual amount necessary for a family of three. Collect their answers and report back the range and the average or median. How does the poverty standard today support or conflict with these numbers?

4. Ask the class to assess the recent trends in child support enforcement. What progress has been made? How do students assess the interest in "deadbeat dads?" Is this a form of "blaming the victim? Look at the US Census Bureau's information online (note 39) regarding fathers in the lowest income quartile; how do students interpret this finding?

5. The information on children in poverty and the elderly can be supplemented with statistics on trends in federal social welfare spending on the two groups. The Green Book publishes data that indicates that spending on the elderly (per aged person) is more than four times spending on each child. Ask students to brainstorm reasons. Contrast the costs of a nursing home patient covered by Medicaid with the cost of providing well child-care under the Child Health Insurance Program (CHIP).

6. Use the section on urban and rural poverty to explore poverty issues in the various areas where the students work or are in practicum.

7. The section on work and poverty illustrates the dynamic nature of social welfare in the context of the U.S. economy. Have students study the prevailing wage rates for entry-level jobs. National newspapers regularly report on labor trends, particularly when legislation around the minimum wage is being debated. Another excellent source is the <u>Monthly Labor Review</u>. Note that minimum wage workers earn approximately $10,000 for full-time, full-year work.

8. The "Living Wage Movement" and other strategies to "make work pay" are important policy goals. To a great extent, federal policy is most important here in setting a national standard; however, there are opportunities for state and local policy work as well, and some states and cities have adopted higher minimum wages. The authors note in Table 5.5, States with Minimum Wages above the Federal Rate, that poverty rates vary widely in the U.S. This information points to the further need for living wage standards.

9. Obtain a copy of Barbara Ehrenreich's *Nickel and Dimed*. Have students read this book and comment on implications to living wage policy that this text suggests.

10. Have students brainstorm individually a list of their living expenses versus the poverty line wage maximum. What activities or expenses should be "sacrificed?" Hold a group discussion regarding whether or not asking the impoverished to "sacrifice" is ethical.

Classroom Discussion Questions

1. What feasible strategies do you suggest for reducing poverty? Be specific. What policies and programs would you change? How?

2. Do the Culture of Poverty elements discriminate against certain races and ethnicities or are the reasons given legitimate elements of poverty?

3. What are some of your ideas regarding how to remedy the situations of the working poor population?

4. How can social workers combat the fringe economy most effectively?

5. How can the "War on Poverty" achieve bipartisan support? What would you do if you were in the position to change legislation to achieve this?

Spotlight Box

The living wage is a controversial topic. Arguments for and against raising the minimum wage are compelling and it may be difficult to ascertain which "side of the fence" is correct. Visit www.financeprojectinfo.org/WIN/wages.asp and read differing opinions, deciding for yourself which is more compelling. Encourage your students to locate other on-line, up-to-date resources for this debate.

Chapter 6   The Voluntary Sector Today

Chapter Overview

This chapter discusses the voluntary sector and its legacy in American social welfare, as well as the role it plays in advancing social justice in contemporary social work practice. A case is made for a present-day re-emergence of the voluntary sector in light of political pressures for less government, coupled with calls for the voluntary sector to shoulder more of the welfare burden. Domains of organized response to human need are described relative to their focus on social issues and the populations that they serve. The assets and service focus of major nonprofit organizations are compared, and the future of the voluntary sector is discussed in terms of commercialism, faith-based initiatives, and social entrepreneurship.

Learning Objectives

1. The reluctance of taxpayers and politicians to authorize major new government expenditures has created a new emergence of the voluntary sector in the US.

2. The voluntary sector is truly one of the first modern vestiges of welfare institution in the US. The four subgroups which hold responsibility in contemporary society for the welfare of society are the traditional providers, welfare bureaucrats, clinical entrepreneurs, and humans service organization executives.

3. Following the New Deal, influence and importance of the voluntary sector waned. During the 1980's when government began to take less control of the social service industry, the voluntary sector reemerged strongly.

4. The voluntary sector has not been seen as a 'major player' until recently in the provision of services to TANF program clients. This re-discovery of the voluntary sector is a reminder to re-double efforts to 'think out of the box' for solutions. It is all too easy to become complacent with the status quo and not look beyond current service delivery approaches for provision options in the other provider domains.

5. United States citizens have had a history of generously donating to nonprofit organizations. Can the voluntary sector provide the level of social services that federal, state, and local governments presently offer? Probably not. However, there will always be a role for the voluntary sector in assisting present providers to sustain and hopefully to increase the level of services provided to those in need.

6. Philanthropic giving is a reminder that policy does not exist in a vacuum. Elite, and to a lesser extent, bourgeois philanthropy, take advantage of provisions in the U. S. Tax Code which make donations partially- or wholly-deductible. Social policy exists in a cultural, economic, and political milieu which encourages/discourages social outcomes.

7. Faith-based services have been an integral part of the provider fabric in U. S. welfare history. For decades service agencies operated by religious denominations have been recipients of tax-based reimbursements and grants for the provision of social services. In terms of revenue sources these agencies are quasi-public.

8. Impropriety within non profit organizations does cause a dip in public support, as seen in the United Way scandal of the 1990's and more recently giving to causes associated with the various 9/11 funds.

9. Social entrepreneurship describes a trend that attempts to harness the synergy between private and nonprofit collaborations with the resulting efforts benefiting a community or client population. Social work must be open to these cutting-edge initiatives as being one more avenue by which to address social justice issues.

Teaching Suggestions and Exercises for Student Learning

1. Select a social issue dealing with a marginalized population that cuts across all four of the provider sectors (traditional providers, welfare bureaucrats, clinical entrepreneurs, and human services executives). Examples of issues would be: addictions, permanency planning for children, and mental health. Divide the class into groups assigning each group an issue. Combining field interviews with agency professionals and journal/book –based research, each group should compile best practices of their particular provider sector relative to the social issue selected. Examples of unresolved challenges faced by their sector in providing services to that population (funding, public apathy, lack of resources, non-existent policy, etc.) should be noted as well.

2. Visit a local foundation. Find out who they fund. If feasible, have the class complete a grant application to address a documented need in the community.

3. Invite your local Title XX administrator to class to discuss the non-profit organizations (including faith-based agencies) that are currently receiving Title XX funding.

4. Select any social problem in contemporary United States society. Discuss the history of voluntary agencies attempting to address the underlying issues of the problem selected.

5. Using the same social problem selected in the previous question, discuss GOVERNMENTAL attempts to address the underlying issues of the problem. Discuss any differences in focus, values, and success between the two helping sectors.

6. Discuss the similarities/differences between the beliefs of 'compassionate conservatism' and the schools of political thought outlined in Chapter 1 of the text. How do these beliefs fit with the values of social work?

7. Select any social problem in contemporary United States society. Discuss the differences in focus that a traditional provider versus a clinical entrepreneur may have in the resolution of that problem. Discuss the benefits of combining the strengths of these two providers in resolving the problem.

8. Identify examples of 'elite' and 'bourgeois' philanthropy in your community. Apply the concepts of 'social justice' and 'marginalized population' to your examples.

9. Select any social issue in our society. Discuss how social entrepreneurship could address unmet needs. What would be some of the factors that would hinder the growth of social entrepreneurship initiatives?

10. Obtain a copy of your local United Way's community needs assessment. Determine in what areas of philanthropy your community is succeeding and in what areas it needs additional support.

Classroom Discussion Questions

1. Discuss the political and economic circumstances that gave rise to the present day re-emergence of the voluntary sector.

2. Can the voluntary sector replace today's governmental social programs? Discuss how other countries deliver social services.

3. What are the ethical and value issues of a social worker in private practice?

4. Can charitable giving replace federal social welfare? Why or why not?

5. After looking at United Way's community needs assessment (Teaching Suggestion #10), are there any needs about which you feel especially passionate? How would you create a nonprofit to meet these needs?

Spotlight Box

The December 2004 tsunami that devastated Southeast Asia was an opportunity for the voluntary sector to emerge as a strong support mechanism. According to USAid.com, almost $1 billion was raised in the US alone through private donations to assist relief and aid efforts. Organizations such as Action Against Hunger, American Red Cross, AmeriCares, Asia Foundation, BAPS Care International, CARE, Habitat for Humanity International, Islamic Relief Worldwide, Save the Children, UNICEP, World Vision and the World Food Programme, among others, offer volunteerism and funding to aid in relief and rebuilding efforts. Visit www.charitynavigator.org to read about how funds are raised, disseminated, and spent for disaster relief and aid efforts. This site also serves as a watchdog for illegitimate fundraising practices.

Chapter 7

Privatization and Human Service Corporations

Chapter Overview

The corporate sector has come to health and human service delivery. This chapter describes how free enterprise affects service delivery and public opinion in this area. While the authors describe a changing and complex environment, one point is made very clear...the conservatism in our federal government is responsible for the privatization of health and human services. This chapter continues to expand from one edition to the next, just as privatization has spread, and is richly referenced with 175 end notes.

Learning Objectives

1. Historically, social welfare was largely the province of the public and not-for-profit sectors. Since 1980 there has been a growing political and economic interest in "privatizing" public services. Some of this interest is rooted in the view that the private sector is more efficient than the public sector.

2. Privatization reflects the pluralist nature of American culture and the plural influences on American social welfare policy.

3. Anti-government, pro-business sentiment fueled privatization in the 1980's.

4. The creation of the President's Commission on Privatization (1988) illustrates the public and private support for and the importance of the concept. The Commission identified three approaches to privatizing service delivery: 1) selling government assets, 2) contracting out services, and 3) using vouchers.

5. Since federal, state and local governments spend a conservative estimate of $500 billion a year paying public workers to deliver goods and services, the potential scope of privatization is significant.

6. Many health and human service professionals question the value of privatization, and the authors note that some research on for-profit firms supports such questioning.

7. Since the passage of PRWORA, some states have experimented with privatizing public welfare. Texas was the first state to allow a private company to administer welfare. Major firms including IBM, Lockheed Martin, Electronic Data Systems, and Anderson Consulting were involved.

8. Privatization issues emphasized by the authors include: corporatization, commercialization, preferential selection, cost-effectiveness, standardization, and oligopolization.

9. Health care is one of the most prominent examples of privatization given the extent of the existing health goods and services that are controlled by the private sector. For example, consider pharmaceuticals, health insurance, HMO's, and nursing homes.

10. Unions play a significant role in privatization; AFSCME has 55,000 social workers as members, and SEIU has 26,000. Given the declining percent of the labor force that is unionized, this is even more remarkable.

11. The authors contend that the full extent of corporate actions related to social welfare is "underappreciated, expanding…(and) not well documented." I believe this is a very important point. While business enterprises are accustomed to thinking about market share, marketing, and expansion opportunities, many social workers lose sight of larger issues and their consequences.

12. Table 7.2, Private Social Welfare Expenditures, helps put in perspective trends in private social welfare expenditures from 1980-1994. As percent of GDP, private SWE grew much more rapidly than public.

13. The authors' connect the privatization issue to the broader issue of the need for national industrial policy and the related issues of human capital investment and individual social welfare.

14. Figure 7.1, Human Service Corporations Reporting Annual Revenues, shows a rapid growth in human service corporations with annual revenues above $10 million; the number grew by almost 800 percent between 1981 and 2000, though some decrease is noted in 2003.

15. Table 7.5, Prominent Health and Human Service Firms, illustrates the concentration of firms in the health care sector; instructors should note the connection between this material and the chapter on the American health care system.

16. The last chapter shows the growth of privatization in selected service areas: nursing homes, hospitals, HMO's, child care, and corrections. Taken as a whole, the scope of privatization of health and human services is vast.

Teaching Suggestions and Exercises for Student Learning

1. Many students may be unfamiliar with the issue of "auspices" and its potential influence on social welfare. I would start with clarification of the three sectors: public, private not-for-profit or nonprofit, and private for-profit or proprietary. It may be necessary to provide legal definitions and to distinguish between "making a profit" and distributing a profit. Organizational maintenance is at work in all sectors, for better and for worse.

2. A formula that I use repeatedly in exploring social policy issues, borrowed from the British social policy scholar Richard Rose is: **TWS= S+M+F**--or the **T**otal **W**elfare of any **S**ociety is a function of what the **S**tate (or government or public sector does) plus the **M**arket (broadly defined as the market in which buyers and sellers exchange goods and services) plus the **F**amily (which in some cases provides services and in other cases purchases services, depending on labor force participation). Much can be done with this formula. International comparisons are particularly appropriate.

3. Compare policies related to labor, child care, and family and medical leave with policies of other OECD countries using the TWS formula above.

4. To follow the developing trends in privatization, note the wide variety of reference sources in the authors' end notes.

5. Suggest that students discuss the issue of privatization with those directly involved: owners, managers, workers and clients/patients of privatized services.

6. Have the class discuss reasons for policy instruction as it relates to privatization.

7. As David Donnison has suggested, welfare professionals would be wise to reconsider their aversion to the private sector and to try to find the "progressive potential in privatization." What does this mean to you?

8. Organize a classroom debate regarding privatization. Have half of the students argue for privatization and the other half argue against the practice. Encourage your students to do background research into the "side" they will argue prior to the classroom debate.

9. Discuss the pros and cons of corporate welfare.

10. How does the concept of corporate social responsibility play out in your community. Invite a community relations officer from a corporation in your area to come and speak about their commitment to the local and global community.

Classroom Discussion Questions

1. Why do some assume that unions are harmful? Why do some assume that unions are helpful? To what extent is anti-union sentiment at work in privatization proposals?

2. What are the fundamental questions/concerns regarding privatization?

3. Are the objectives "to make a profit" and "to perform a public service" fundamentally incompatible?

4. Why do some consider professional practice within a corporate context antithetical to the very idea of "social" welfare? What do you believe regarding this issue?

5. As a future social worker, how do you feel regarding privatization? What "works?" What doesn't "work?"

Spotlight Box

Corrections Corporation of America is the sixth largest corrections system in the nation, behind only the federal government and four states. An example of a privatized prison system, more information regarding CCA can we found at www.correctionscorp.com.

Chapter 8

The Making of Governmental Policy

Chapter Overview

This chapter will provide students with a succinct description of the complex process by which governmental policy is made. Particular attention is paid to the phases of this process, as well as social, political, and organizational influences that affect how social policy is interpreted, researched, implemented and evaluated. Various philosophical theories are addressed, including historical social theorists and reform movements that have shaped our current social welfare policy.

Learning Objectives

1. Public policy in the United States is made through a deliberative process that involves elected officials representing their constituents.

2. Only about 5% of the tens of thousands of bills presented in Congress each year ever become law. The process of enacting a policy proposal into law is described as "lengthy and tortuous."

3. Political Action Committees (PACs) and professional lobbyists represent a "big business," with millions spent every year to influence the process of lawmaking.

4. Underrepresented groups, minority groups, and impoverished populations are often left out of the lawmaking process because of their lack of political influence and funding for lobbyists and PACs. The authors provide a section on social stratification, helping to cement the conceptualization of this ideal.

5. The context of the economic system and the idea of market rationality are very influential in US lawmaking process.

6. The major government think tanks, GAO, CBO, CRS, and OMB are described in the section on evaluation.

7. The authors provide a section on Social Workers and Social Reform which discusses social workers' roles in the formulation of policy and the advocacy that must take place in order for effective policy to become law.

Teaching Suggestions and Exercises for Student Learning

1. Start out the class and ascertain students' opinions regarding the creation/passage of social welfare policies. At the end of the chapter discussion, reevaluate how opinions and/or initial impressions may have changed.

2. Have students discuss the following statement from the text: "The discrepancy between what is constitutionally prescribed in making public policy and the way decisions are actually made leads to two quite different understandings of the policy process." What does this mean?

3. In preparing students for the role of policy advocate, obtain a copy of *Robert's Rules of Order* and have students identify rules pertaining specifically to the legislative process.

4. Retrieve the House Ways and Means Committee's *Green Book* online or through your legislator. Throughout the semester, have the students reference the *Green Book* for facts and figures when discussing various social programs.

5. Contact a local chapter of one of the PAC contributors listed in Table 8.3, Top PAC Contributors. Determine how and where expenditures were placed for the last fiscal year.

6. Have your class read Albert O. Hirschman's *Shifting Involvements* and discuss the author's suggested implications for private and public interests.

7. Look up the "Presidential Management Fellows" program online. Have students determine for what positions they may be qualified. Encourage your students to apply for these fellowships following the completion of their degree program.

8. Have students prepare a biographical profile on a leader of the social reform movement, as mentioned in Chapter 8. Encourage students to take a psychosocial approach in their research surrounding this leader and postulate as to what environmental and societal influences led to their development as one of social work's "greats."

9. Have your class identify social work practitioners who are currently in the political arena, as either elected legislators, or assistants/consultants to legislators. Contact those in your area and arrange for one or more to provide a guest lecture.

10. Using the groups established for Chapter 2 activities, have each Small Learning Group choose a policy or program and evaluate it using the following criteria: Adequacy, Equity, Economy, Efficiency, and Effectiveness.

Classroom Discussion Questions

1. How can campaign financing be effectively and fairly reformed?

2. What should our role as social workers be in the lobbying process? How can we be effective lobbyists? What reforms are needed?

3. Why do you think the poor and young are less likely to vote?

4. Jane Addams said of social work, "It must decide whether its to remain behind in the area of caring for the victimized, or whether to press ahead into the dangerous area of conflict where the struggle must be pressed to bring to pass an order of society with few victims." How are we, as professionals, living up to her charge?

5. "There are increasing numbers of non-social workers, including psychologists and urban planners, taking what might have been social work jobs in service delivery and policy analysis." What does Eleanor Brilliant's statement mean to the profession of social work? For you as a future practitioner?

Spotlight Box

Together, the authors of this text founded policyAmerica, a nonprofit organization dedicated to disseminating innovations in social policy. That organization's website, www.policyamerica.org, lists several policy initiatives for students to consider. What issues are most interesting and/or pertinent to you and your community?

Chapter 9

Tax Policy and
Income Distribution

Chapter Overview

This chapter emphasizes the role of tax policy in income distribution and explains its significance in American social welfare. The authors review the history of US tax policy, and they explain key concepts such as *progressive* and *regressive* taxes. The different types of taxes are described in the context of the federal budget. International comparisons are facilitated with historical and contemporary OECD data. The relationship between taxation and family income distribution is elucidated and concepts about tax expenditures explained.

Learning Objectives

1. Tax policy is constantly changing and of increasing importance to advocates for social justice.

2. The welfare state was effectively created in 1935 by the Social Security Act.

3. There is widespread opposition to many tax proposals and the elections of President Ronald Reagan, George Bush, and George W. Bush exemplify the popularity of anti-tax sentiment in favor of tax cuts.

4. Created by the 16th amendment, the federal income tax is just one component of American tax policy. The withholding tax and Earned Income Tax Credit have also become a very important component of social welfare policy, providing support for millions of low-income Americans.

5. Social Security is a regressive tax, and most taxpayers now pay more in Social Security taxes than in income taxes.

6. Table 9.1, Distribution of Federal Taxes by Quintiles, shows how low U.S. taxes are in comparison with most OECD countries.

7. Social insurance programs, such as Social Security and Medicare, tend to make the biggest dent in poverty in the U.S.

8. The authors discuss the role of tax policy in reducing poverty, and they document the variation in state income taxes on low-income families (pages 240-244).

9. Tax expenditures are explained. This concept is confusing to many students.

10. The discussion of the anti-tax movement illustrates the importance of American public opinion in social policy.

11. Upward mobility in the U.S. appears to be substantial and increasing. Between 25% and 40% of the population move into a new, higher income quintile each year.

Teaching Suggestions and Exercises for Student Learning

1. Have your class debate the necessity and equity of having the top quintile pay a majority of taxes that support social programs.

2. To illustrate the complexity of the US tax code, obtain a copy from your university library and have students reference various laws pertaining to social welfare programs.

3. Obtain a copy of the *New York Times* article "Corporate Welfare's New Enemies." Discuss the article in class and encourage students to critically analyze assumptions in the article.

4. Find out if agencies in your areas offer free tax preparation services to financially "strapped" individuals. Suggest that students volunteer their services for this agency, depending on their abilities.

5. The EITC has often been lauded as one of, if not THE most successful Federal welfare program. Others completely disagree. Have students postulate as to reasons that proponents and adversaries of the program would hold their separate opinions.

6. Have your class, regardless of political persuasion; divide into two groups representing the liberal and conservative viewpoints regarding government taxation. Stage a debate and ask students at the end of the class which arguments are most convincing for each side.

7. Invited students to retrieve current articles and clippings addressing the continuous political debates regarding tax cuts. Discuss the viewpoints of each side utilizing article information.

8. Ask students if they have ever noticed FICA, OASDI, or HI on their pay stubs. The text notes that most taxpayers pay more in these types of taxes than in income taxes today. Ask students to ask research if this was true two decades ago.

9. Ask students to suggest policy changes. Evaluate the economic and political feasibility of the proposed changes.

10. Ask the students to guess which of the two major political parties in the U.S. has been most responsible for the social programs of the New Deal and Great Society. Usually, they will say that the Democratic Party was more active in promoting those policies and programs. Then I tell the story of the Republican operative in the late 1970's who expressed concern that "the Democrats have convinced the American people that the Democrats alone have been responsible for all of those helpful programs while the Republicans have done nothing." (Obviously, the instructor needs to be careful and sensitive if choosing to use this example.) The Republican operative proposed that the Republican Party develop a *Two Santa Claus* theory of politics. Since social programs have to be paid for, Republicans would contend that they would present themselves as the 2nd Santa Claus—a different Santa Claus. They would let the Democrats be the Santa Claus of giving people social programs; the Republicans would remind the citizens that programs cost money and would become the Santa Claus of giving people tax cuts. Over the past twenty years the campaign behavior of the two parties has frequently followed this approach.

Classroom Discussion Questions

1. What do you think President Ronald Reagan meant by his proposal to "get the government off the back" of the American taxpayer or President George Bush's pledge to not say the "T" word? How has this affected our nation today?

2. Why do you think the U.S. allocates a much greater sum to subsidize housing for the middle-income than to subsidize housing for the poor?

3. Given that most social workers vote Democratic, does this affect social workers' lobbying efforts? Note that in recent elections, African Americans have also disproportionately supported Democratic candidates for the Presidency. Has this affected the ability of African American lobbying groups to effectively lobby Republican candidates?

4. Since 1980, inequality of income distribution has increased. Can this trend continue in the same direction?

5. Debt changed from 1980-1992 and from 1992-2001. What caused debt to rise dramatically in the 1980's and then eventually decline in the 1990's?

Spotlight Box

The Human Development Report (HDR) was first launched in 1990 with the single goal of putting people back at the center of the development process in terms of economic debate, policy and advocacy. Since the first Report, four new composite indices for human development have been developed — the Human Development Index, the Gender-related Development Index, the Gender Empowerment Measure, and the Human Poverty Index. Visit http://hdr.undp.org/reports/global/2004/ to read the 2004 Human Development Report.

Chapter 10   Social Insurance Programs

Chapter Overview

This chapter examines the major forms of social insurance in the United States: Old-Age, Survivors, and Disability Insurance (OASDI), Unemployment Insurance (UI), and Workers' Compensation. In addition to discussing some of the major issues and problems facing social insurance programs, the authors refer to and expound upon the fact that our country's social insurance programs are the "cornerstone of US social welfare policy." This section also discusses some of the proposed solutions for Social Security problems, with an in-depth analysis of pros and cons of each proposal.

Learning Objectives

1. Social insurance programs serve as insurance against the possibility of indigence for almost 40 million Americans.

2. Social insurance programs are funded at more than twice the level of public welfare, contrary to what many citizens believe. There is little stigma attached to the utilization of social insurance programs because it is linked to occupationally defined productive work.

3. The history of worldwide social insurance programs is usually traced to 1889 and the first old-age insurance program introduced in Germany by Chancellor Otto von Bismarck.

4. The authors briefly describe the passage of the Social Security Act in 1935. It had many opponents as well as supporters, and the legislation had to survive two Supreme Court challenges to remain law. Many historians have described the fights between FDR and the Supreme Court of the 1930's.

5. The number of beneficiaries is now approximately 40 million, and this number will rise steadily as the "baby boomers" generation begins to retire between 2008-2111. The number of workers per beneficiary is projected to decline from 3.4 in 2000 to about 2 in 2032.

6. The various social insurance programs are defined and discussed in detail and an emphasis should be placed on the differences between OASDI, UI, and Workers' Compensation. OASDI recipients will not be treated any differently than a beneficiary of like circumstances who happens to live in another state. UI is different; it varies considerably by state.

7. Unlike European UI benefits, US benefits replace smaller percentages of income (average 47% in 2003). The authors describe the program's many problems, starting with the fact, "In 2003, only 44 percent of unemployed persons received benefits."

8. The Workers Compensation program also varies considerably from state to state. WC problems are similar to UI problems. A particular WC problem is the long delay between time of injury and time of benefits. If the state has a Temporary Disability Insurance program (few states do), this can help. Employers may also have private insurance programs.

9. The authors introduce an extensive section on the problems of the Social Security program. The 2000 report estimates that OASI trust funds will be exhausted in 2039.

Teaching Suggestions and Exercises for Student Learning

1. Here is a trick question that usually produces surprising answers. Ask students to *estimate* the percentage of Social Security expenditures that toward administrative expenditures. Put the students' estimates on the blackboard in a range from low to high. Do not be surprised if a student guesses 50 percent or higher. Summarize the guesses for a class vote; for example, include the lowest guess, the highest guess and one in between. Ask the students to pick one by a show of hands and put the vote count beside the estimates. Tell the students that the administrative expenditures vary by program as follows:

   Administrative Expenses as percentage of the GDP, 2000
   - OASI: .005 (that is, ½ of 1%)
   - Disability Insurance: 3%
   - Health Insurance: 1.4%

   Source: "Summary of the 2000 Annual Social Security and Medicare Trust Fund Reports," *Social Security Bulletin*, Vol. 63, No. 1, 2000, page 54.

2. From the following example, ask students to discuss the following questions in groups of four and create a classroom discussion surrounding their answers: Why do people assume Social Security expenditures are so high? What does this say about the image of the program? If social work students guess high, what will ordinary citizens guess? Why are expenditures much higher in some programs than other (degree of eligibility monitoring)? Instructors can also introduce the contrasting high administrative costs of public assistance programs.

3. Bring in a copy of the *Social Security Bulletin* and/or an article from one.

4. Debate any of the variety of contemporary issues surrounding Social Security: privatization, means-testing, COLA modification, etc. The annual issue of the *Budget Options* book from the Congressional Budget Office (CBO) is a good resource for this and other revenue and expenditure policy options.

5. Refer to the *Green Book*; bring in a copy from your university's library reference section. If the Library does not have a copy, recommend that they obtain at least one from a recent year. This is a tremendous resource for students doing work in any of the covered program areas. However, the amount of data can be overwhelming; some recent issues are 2000 pages long.

6. Bring in a Social Security worker, supervisor, or administrator to discuss current issues. Students should know the importance of these programs, how many beneficiaries and dependents there are, basic eligibility rules, and enough about the delivery system to be able to refer potentially eligible recipients. Students do not need to become experts in social insurance policy, but they should know enough to make referrals and to recognize the need for appeals and case advocacy.

7. Bring in a copy of any CBO report on entitlement programs.

8. Copy the page/table "CBO Projections of Mandatory Spending…" from the annual CBO Report, The Budget and Economic Outlook: Fiscal Years 2001-2010. This provides a useful summary of federal spending on the social insurance and public assistance programs.

9. Use any contemporary debate/discussion/legislative initiative/newspaper series to demonstrate the importance of the Social Security issue. To utilize pertinent information, bring in clips from Congressional Hearings. C-SPAN, the Cable Satellite Public Affairs Network is a primary source. C-SPAN has a generous copyright policy that permits copying for educational purposes.

10. Have your class debate possible solutions for the current Social Security debacle.

Classroom Discussion Questions

1. What is the most important problem facing Social Security? Utilize a "pre-test/post-test" method to determine how student answers vary before and after class lecture and reading.

2. What are the advantages and disadvantages of Social Security privatazation? Who might win; who might lose? How does this issue change with the ups and downs of the equities markets?

3. Is Social Security still "The Third Rail of Politics"? What is the meaning of this expression?

4. Does the scope of social insurance spending affect the inadequacy of funding for children's programs? (Note: Generational conflict should be avoided as much as possible. In recent years, advocacy and interest groups representing children and the elderly [CDF and AARP, for example] have tried to work together.)

5. Aside from advocating for political involvement and action, what can social workers do to remedy Social Security problems for individual clients?

Spotlight Box

Each year the Trustees of the Social Security and Medicare trust funds report on the current status and projected condition of the funds over the next 75 years. Their website, www.ssa.gov/OACT/TRSUM/trsummary.html, denotes that Social Security and Medicare remain problematic economically and estimates that "growing deficits in both programs will lead to exhaustion in trust fund reserves for HI in 2020 and for Social Security in 2041. We do not believe the currently projected long run growth rates of Social Security and Medicare are sustainable under current financing arrangements." Continue to browse this report and find other interesting "factoids" that may not be seen as public information. Share these with your class and discuss the implications.

Chapter 11   Public Assistance Programs

Chapter Overview

This is one of the most important chapters in the book. It describes the major public assistance programs and the ways these programs have changed in recent years. Additionally, authors provide a wonderful and informative section on some of the most prominent myths regarding public opinion of public assistance programs. A major focus is the transition from AFDC to TANF in 1996 and the distinguishing characteristics of each program. Contemporary issues surrounding all forms of public assistance are discussed, including current debates centered on welfare reform and what that term entails for conservatives vs. liberals, etc. The chapter also explores key welfare reform issues: teenage pregnancy, the underclass, welfare behaviorism, and welfare to work. Throughout the chapter, the authors document the inadequacy of benefits and the problems arising from this imbalance.

Learning Objectives

1. Figure 11.1, Where Federal Dollars Go, puts public assistance programs in perspective in regard to federal dollars spent. In 2003, much less than 10% of federal expenditures were spent on these programs, in sharp contrast to almost 30% alone on defense, and 20% going toward interest on the national debt.

2. The authors note the conflicting American attitudes and feelings over public assistance. Sometimes the attitudes are compassionate and charitable; at other times they are hostile and mean-spirited. Many of the attitudes are based on misinformation and misunderstandings.

3. The various myths detailed in Chapter 11 point to errant beliefs in a variety of areas, including age and gender of welfare recipients, percentage of cash assistance, size of families receiving welfare, length of time on welfare, etc

4. The authors draw on much of the research from the Institute for Research on Poverty. There is a massive amount of detail beyond the explanations in the text.

5. The history of AFDC and the enactment of TANF are major developments in social welfare. President Clinton had vetoed welfare reform legislation in 1995. As the authors note, the Personal Responsibility and Work Opportunity Reconciliation Act of 1996 was "a complex 900-page document that confused even seasoned welfare administrators."

6. There is a very long section in this chapter describing individual state projects. One of the disadvantages of TANF and devolution in general is the reliance on state initiatives and the ensuing unequal treatment of clients in different states.

Teaching Suggestions and Exercises for Student Learning

1. Many of the myths discussed in this chapter would be useful for class debate and quizzes.

2. Create a focus on the variety of initiatives and particular programs in states where your students will work. This is a particularly useful exercise if the students in your classroom are from a cross-section of areas.

3. Commit a special lecture to the discussion of welfare as understood through the lenses of the NASW Code of Ethics. Remind students that the code speaks of "promoting the general welfare" and acting to "prevent and eliminate...exploitation...and discrimination."

4. If the class has limited welfare experience, ask them to brainstorm what they believe "welfare" to be. Explore denotative and connotative definitions. Many citizens think of welfare as the AFDC/TANF program. Ask students to "guess-timate" how much the federal government spends on this program. Produce current information that corrects any errant information the students might hold.

5. Have students survey a random sample of family, friends, and persons on the street about opinions, attitudes and understanding of "welfare." Compare these responses to the class' initial responses.

6. Discuss the average benefit amounts in various states including those in your university's region.

7. Invite a supervisor or experienced worker from the agency that administers TANF to speak to the class. Ask the speaker to describe the job of an *eligibility determination worker*, including information about Quality Control regulations. If the supervisor knows of clients who would be willing to talk about their experiences with AFDC or TANF, consider inviting the clients.

8. Historically, AFDC eligibility and services were connected. One worker determined eligibility for financial benefits and also developed a "prescribed services plan" for each member of the family. This was changed in the 1960's when welfare rights advocates argued that those in financial need should not be assumed to need services. Thereafter, local welfare departments separated eligibility and services; many states re-classified positions and hired eligibility workers. Prescribed services were no longer automatic. Gradually, social service units in many states began to focus on child welfare programs after families developed sufficient problems to require state intervention. Ask students to evaluate the consequences of this policy change. Relate this discussion to the chapter on child welfare.

9. Discuss the current research undertaken by the Urban Institute under the *Assessing the New Federalism* project. There are special studies on the effects of TANF and broader studies of family economic well-being. Another important think-tank on this topic is the Center on Budget and Policy Priorities. CBPP produces many different types of reports, and they frequently are invited to testify on Congressional policy proposals.

10. Acquire GAO documents on the impact of welfare reform and share them with students. Also acquire the annual HHS TANF Reports to Congress. In recent years, these have been published near the end of the Fiscal Year.

Classroom Discussion Questions

1. Contrast SSI and TANF. Remind students that when SSI was created as a primarily federal program, AFDC had been considered for the same action. What are the consequences? Would it be useful to consider some national standard for TANF?

2. Why are public assistance programs more controversial than their more expensive social insurance program counterparts?

3. What are the implications of the problem of teenage pregnancy to social workers? How can we work with clients to ameliorate the issues associated with teen pregnancy, while still recognizing and allowing for client self-determination?

4. How do social workers define the underclass? How is this different from how other professions might define it?

5. You are elected "President for the Day." What immediate actions will you take to reform welfare, if any?

Spotlight Box

Recently marriage has become a national issue of public policy in the United States. The Bush Administration has proposed that the Federal government dedicate $300 million a year as part of the Temporary Assistance for Needy Families (TANF) program to "help couples form and sustain healthy marriages." Proposed legislation focuses on eight allowable activities:

1. Public advertising campaigns on the value of marriage and the skills needed to increase marital stability and health.
2. Education in high schools on the value of marriage, relationship skills, and budgeting.
3. Marriage education, marriage skills, and relationship skills programs, which may include parenting skills, financial management, conflict resolution, and job and career advancement, for non-married pregnant women and non-married expectant fathers.
4. Pre-marital education and marriage skills training for engaged couples and for couples or individuals interested in marriage.
5. Marriage enhancement and marriage skills training programs for married couples.
6. Divorce reduction programs that teach relationship skills.
7. Marriage mentoring programs, which use married couples as role models and mentors.
8. Programs to reduce the disincentives to marriage in means-tested aid programs, if offered in conjunction with any activity described in this subparagraph.

Source: *Personal Responsibility, Work, and Family Promotion Act of 2003. H.R.4.IH*

Chapter 12

The American
Health Care System

Chapter Overview

This chapter describes the American health care system and the extraordinary changes that have taken place over the past twenty years. It describes the major public programs, the importance of the private sector, and the unique character of the American system in comparison with other industrial nations, including pros and cons for America's system.

This chapter also introduces a major problem: America's uninsured population. Despite the fact that the US spends 19% of all government expenditures each year on health care alone, 45 million Americans still do not have health insurance. A complete review of the chapter makes it clear that there are no easy solutions to this problem and there are many problems beyond the lack of health insurance coverage for some.

Learning Objectives

1. In 2003, both the number of insured and uninsured in the US rose. Approximately 16% of the public does not have health care coverage and a large proportion of those are children.

2. The average insurance premium for families in 2004 was $9,320; that number is expected to rise to over $14,500 by the year 2006.

3. The absence of health insurance has serious consequences for both the uninsured and American taxpayers. It is estimated that medical care for the uninsured in 2001 cost almost $100 billion. Additionally, Americans without insurance cost the economy between $65-130 billion every year in lost productivity.

4. There are five major components to the US health care system, including: physicians in solo practice, group outpatient settings, hospitals, public health services, and corollary health systems (ex: home health care, nursing homes, etc.).

5. Almost 20% of the US population is covered by Medicare or Medicaid. Ensure that your students understand the difference between the two programs; one memory aid technique: Care for the elderly; aid to the needy.

6. Medicare finances are handled by two trust funds n the US Treasury, one for the health insurance program (Part A) and the other for Supplemental Medical Insurance (Part C).

7. Medicaid is a means-tested public assistance program with complicated policies that vary among states.

8. S-CHIP, the State Children's Health Insurance Program implemented in 1997, allocated $48 billion over ten years to expand health care coverage to uninsured children under age 19.

9. The tobacco settlement case requires the tobacco companies to pay $206 billion to 46 states over 25 years. This was the largest settlement in US history.

10. The US is currently in a health care crisis, which the authors discuss in great detail in this chapter.

11. Health care costs in the US are higher than in any other industrialized company.

12. Some of the reasons given for the high cost of US health care include: medical malpractice, treatment of people with AIDS, development of medical technology, insurance costs, increased longevity of citizenry, hospital costs, physician's salaries, and the high cost of pharmaceutics.

13. Ways to solve the health care crisis are often controversial. Possible solutions are offered by the authors in the chapter, representing both a conservative and liberal approach. These include socialized medicine, a national health insurance program, managed care, incremental reform.

14. The last section in the chapter discusses the US health care system in comparison to Canada (single-payer system) and Great Britain (socialized medicine).

Teaching Suggestions and Exercises for Student Learning

1. I recommend that instructors encourage students to read the entire chapter very carefully and think about the ways in which the American health care system is reflective of our country's unique approach to social welfare provision.

2. The way the U. S. government responds to the health care needs of its citizen mirrors the American approach to social welfare. The most recent example of this as a national policy debate occurred when President Clinton proposed national health insurance. Small and large businesses organized to lobby against the health care proposal. Advocates appealed to the public interest and the larger social good. At the outset, it looked like a close fight. In retrospect, it is abundantly clear why the health care industry prevailed.

3. Include Johnson and Broder's (1996) *The System: The American Way of Politics at the Breaking Point* on your class reading list. It provides an astute analysis of the inner working of the United States political system as well as an assessment of why and how the Clinton plan failed.

4. Machiavelli said: "There is nothing more difficult to carry out, nor more doubtful of success, nor dangerous to handle, than to initiate a new order of things. For the reformer has enemies in all who profit by the old order and only lukewarm defenders in all those who would profit by the new order…" How can you apply this to the failed Clinton national health care proposal?

5. Invite a local insurance broker to discuss Medigap and other supplemental insurance programs available. Be sure to ask your guest lecturer to discuss the issues surrounding uninsured individuals from a corporate insurance perspective.

6. Have students conduct an actual cost versus charged cost for medical services. (ie: the cost of Tylenol as opposed to what hospitals charge for it). Discuss the implications of such price gouging.

7. Have students determine what a health insurance policy through your university or college health center costs. Ask students to evaluate what services that could be necessary are or are not included. Would such an insurance plan cause one to be considered "underinsured?"

8. Ask students to brainstorm their suggestions for reforming the health care system in the US. List these suggestions on the classroom board and center a class discussion debating the feasibility of each suggestion.

9. Encourage students to consider the pros and cons of a national health insurance program.

10. Invite a hospital administrator from an area county hospital district to discuss the financial and social implications of serving the uninsured population.

Classroom Discussion Questions

1. What does US health care policy says about the American approach to privatization and consolidation in health service markets?

2. Why are uninsured patients more costly than insured patients?

3. What health care entities should the US emulate in seeking to solve the health care crisis?

4. Should pharmaceutical companies be deregulated and non-privatized? Why or why not? What other solutions can you offer that would decrease the costs of medication and medical innovation?

5. What are the political and social barriers to the implementation of a national health insurance program in the US?

Spotlight Box

The Henry J. Kaiser Family Foundation is a non-profit, private operating foundation focusing on the major health care issues facing the nation and has some interesting non-partisan information regarding managed care, the uninsured, Medicare and Medicaid, HIV/AIDS, women and minority health care, and other health care issues facing the US. Visit the foundation's website at www.kff.org to find links, up-to-date statistics, and information regarding potential answers to the health care crisis in the United States.

Chapter 13

Mental Health and
Substance Abuse Policy

Chapter Overview

This chapter introduces important concepts for all future social work practitioners regarding the provision of mental health and substance abuse care and policy implementation. Instructors should ensure that students have a firm grasp of the history and future of mental health and substance abuse policy. The authors provide an excellent section on and special attention should be given to historical court cases and laws that shape current policy. Community Mental Health Centers and the evolution of mental health care in our society today are given important weight and the effects of marginalization due to deinstitutionalization are discussed in great detail. Finally, private practice in these areas, especially by social workers, will provide an interesting platform for spirited discussion and classroom debate.

Learning Objectives

1. The problem of unmet mental health needs, particularly among the low-income, the uninsured or underinsured, and those with severe mental illness were an issue in the early 1800's and continue to be an issue of concern and debate in local and national politics.

2. While the chapter points to some progress over the past ten years, the extent of mental health and substance abuse problems suggests that more policy advocacy is necessary.

3. Further, since many social workers are employed in the delivery system and most social workers are at least indirectly involved in the delivery system, it is necessary to understand the policy issues. The funding of mental health and substance abuse services is also discussed in great detail.

Teaching Suggestions and Exercises for Student Learning

1. Mental health and substance abuse are issues in which current events are likely to provide interesting material from the local to the national level, including evaluations such as the First Surgeon General's Report on Mental Health and the annual reports of the Office of National Drug Control Policy. Print copies of these reports from the internet and distribute them in class.

2. Students could take responsibility for researching persons/issues and providing brief reports to the class. Suggestions for reports are:
   - Dorothea Dix
   - President Franklin Pierce
   - Community Mental Health Centers Act of 1963
   - President John F. Kennedy
   - Deinstitutionalization
   - Wyatt v. Stickney
   - "The revolving door"
   - Mental Health Parity Act of 1996
   - FAS and FAE
   - Private practice by MSW's
   - YAVIS syndrome
   - EAP's

3. Invite speakers from local mental health advocacy organizations to describe their legislative or service activities.

4. The authors' recommended questions cover history, current problems, and federal to local questions. One area I usually explore is the primary funding sources, how these are changing, and how funding influences "who gets what, when, why, where, and how." I suggest that students look at this for a public mental health agency, a nonprofit service provider, and for an EAP.

5. The authors provide information on treatment episodes in substance abuse; students could compare this data with the data on estimates of incidence of various addictions.

6. Ask students to explore the incidence in the US of various mental illnesses such as major depression and the extent to which these are treated. How has this been changing since the passage of the Mental Health Parity Act of 1996?

7. Ask students if they know of any fictional accounts of mental illness and substance abuse, including novels and films. Recent popular works include Wally Lamb's *I Know This Much is True*, and Susanna Kaysen's (1993) *Girl Interrupted*.

8. Ask students if they know of any nonfictional accounts of mental illness and substance abuse such as novelist William Styron's (1990) *Darkness Visible: A Memoir of Madness*, an account of his battle with depression or former Senator George McGovern's book about his daughter's alcoholism, *Terry: My Daughters Life-and-Death Struggle with Alcoholism*.

9. Obtain a copy of the NIMH's Action For Mental Health (1961). Discuss how the issues surrounding mental health have changed over the past 44 year.

10. Stage a debate focusing on the current "war on drugs." Address issues such as effectiveness, administration, cost, and suggestions for improving or reforming the policy. Additionally, discuss how the legalization of currently-illicit substances would affect this "war."

Classroom Discussion Questions

1. Evaluate the following statement: "for the severely mentally ill, liberty is not just an empty word, but a cruel hoax." What does this mean to you?

2. In what ways could our mental health service delivery system (local, state, and federal) be improved?

3. What are the pros and cons of utilizing a philosophy of harm reduction in substance abuse treatment?

4. How do you feel about the legalizing of currently illicit substances?

5. What are some ethical issues surrounding Social Workers as private practitioners?

Spotlight Box

In the text, Spotlight 13.1 introduces the Substance Abuse and Mental Health Services Administration. An offshoot of this government entity is National Mental Health Information Center, found on the internet at www.mentalhealth.org/cmhs. This website offers interesting information, as well as 30 topics under discussion from substance abuse to psychiatric disorders. Browse this website and pull up current events for your students.

Chapter 14   Criminal Justice

Chapter Overview

This chapter discusses the history of western criminal justice, highlighting pre-modern practices and ideas that influenced the development of the criminal justice system in the United States. Contemporary issues and trends such as the War on Drugs, the underclass and crime, and the 'new penology' are presented in terms of gender, race, and related political and economic factors. Special attention is given to juvenile justice concerns. Boot camps, the adjudication of youthful offenders to adult facilities, and the debate of incarceration versus community-based treatment are also discussed.

Learning Objectives

1. Since the US re-instituted the death penalty in 1976, 56% of those executed were white and 35% black

2. The forced sterilization of prisoners in the 1950's is an example of how easily people who become marginalized by society can suffer injustices without public outrage. It is the responsibility of the profession to assist these populations in developing their political voice.

3. Recent studies indicate that a strong commitment to community alternatives results in lower recidivism rates. The local response to the issue of incarceration vs. alternatives has been mixed, however. On one hand, alternatives to incarceration programs are highlighted by many communities; in sharp contrast however is the telling statistic that the US ranks second only to Russia in the incarceration percentage of its citizens.

4. The War on Drugs policies of interdiction of supply vs. curbing the demand for illegal substances through education highlight how differences in values and point of view can influence subsequent policy and programmatic directions.

5. The 'new penology' philosophy, which concerns itself with the management of inmates, is not unlike the philosophy of institution superintendents in the 1840's. The past 200 years of criminal justice history has seen the policy pendulum swing between punishment and prevention efforts.

6. Communities have used moral, religious, environmental, and psychological arguments to frame their response to crime. Studies indicate a relationship exists between crime and poverty, lack of education opportunities, and drug addiction. Criminal justice is not only a matter of building more prisons or devising state-of-the-art alternative programs. Communities must also look at issues of social and economic justice in the societal, economic, and political milieu for a more holistic response to the complex issues of crime and its prevention.

7. The implementation of policy oftentimes results in unintended effects. The differences in sentencing of those convicted of possession of cocaine versus crack cocaine appear to indicate a racial bias. Social workers have an ethical obligation to analyze the implementation effects of current law through the screens of social and economic justice.

8. As more states are seeking to treat juveniles as adult offenders in terms of due process and sentencing options, the profession must identify and address the justice needs of this fast growing new order of 'adult' offender. The social work educator has a responsibility to prepare students to work with these involuntary clients and their families around issues of support and loss.

Teaching Suggestions and Exercises for Student Learning

1. Have your students consider 'moral poverty' in terms of social justice concerns and the profession's focus on strengths –based interventions. React to the 'conservative prescription for moral poverty' (page761) from the standpoint of a child protection worker.

2. Stage a classroom debate to determine whether certain drugs and controlled substances should be legalized? Discuss in terms of client populations with whom the students are familiar.

3. Have students brainstorm a "compare/contrast" list on the board to discuss the policy focus of the 'new penology' versus the policy focus of incarceration at the time of Dorothea Dix.

4. Hold a classroom discussion regarding new science technologies and the number of death row convicts released from prison due to DNA evidence entered on their behalf. In light of this, should there be a national moratorium on executions?

5. Your class could make a project out of supporting and/or initiating a state-wide "execution moratorium." This would not only enable your students to do policy and statistical research, but act as a foray into political action by writing letters of dissent to state politicians.

6. Via the Internet access state budget documents relative to public expenditures for incarceration-related services and community-based services.

7. If your college or university is located in a larger municipalities or at the county level, interview administrators for information regarding public expenditures for incarceration vs. alternative programming. Students will see how much of the local and state tax dollar goes to support these two issues.

8. Follow on your state's legislative internet site the progress of legislation addressing incarceration or alternative services. Make a class project of contacting key law -makers relative to specific bills.

9. Have students research Boston's Operation Night Light and discuss what components of it might have been responsible for its success. What components of this program are most amenable to a social worker's perspective?

10. Add Dan Baum's *Smoke and Mirrors: The War on Drugs and the Politics of Failure to* your class reading list. Baum is a former journalist and so this book is an interesting and "fast read." Ask students to consider some of Baum's conjecture regarding the efficacy of the War on Drugs.

Classroom Discussion Questions

1. People of color and the poor are disproportionately represented among those who are incarcerated in the United States criminal justice system. Discuss this fact in terms of social work's commitment to social justice and how the profession can make a difference in the criminal justice system.

2. Discuss the differences (if any) that would be evident today in the criminal justice system if President Pierce in 1854 gave the federal government more of a role in the institutional control of prisoners.

3. The practice of involuntarily sterilizing convicts abated during the Civil Rights movement era. Discuss possible reasons why the sterilizations ceased in terms of the influences of the social and political movements in the 1960's.

4. Among the nations of the world, the incarceration rate in the US is second only to that of Russia. Discuss this fact in terms of cost of incarceration vs. less costly community alternatives, concern for public safety, and taking responsibility for one's own actions.

5. In the War on Drugs, two strategies dominated: interdict the supply and treat the addict. If you were a legislator deciding on what programs to fund what evidence could you bring to support a policy course of action?

Spotlight Box

Access the Innocence Project (key word) at www.criminaljustice.org. Another useful site is, www.chartoftheday.com. Select any number of topics highlighted to use as a focus of a class project or discussion. For example, the Indigent Defense topic could spark discussion on the morality of the criminal justice system and our ethical responsibilities to find ways to meet the legal and emotional needs of death row populations.

Chapter 15   Child Welfare Policy

Chapter Overview

In Chapter 15, the authors describe a major field of social work practice—child welfare. The major child welfare program components are child protective services (CPS), foster care and adoption. Many of the public agency child welfare workers in the US are BSW's and MSW's (including the many who start their careers in child welfare <u>before</u> enrolling in a graduate education program).

The history of child welfare programs is traced to the 1870's and the infamous Mary Ellen case. Students usually are intrigued by the pre-existence of the New York Society for the Prevention of Cruelty to Animals. While the New York Society for the Prevention of Cruelty to Children was developed in the 1870's, it is interesting to note that the CAPTA legislation was enacted almost a century later.

Learning Objectives

1. The authors emphasize child poverty as an important context of child welfare. Compare the percent of children who are poor in the US with those in other countries. Child poverty in the US is in stark contrast.

2. The history of child welfare as a problem and as a social service is unusual. The Mary Ellen case illustrates many things including the importance of a social worker's advocacy in the creation of the New York Society for the Prevention of Cruelty to Children.

3. The creation of the US Children's Bureau in 1912 is described. This important agency is still in existence as part of the Department of Health and Human Services, within the Administration of Children, Youth and Families (ACYF). There are other child welfare related divisions and bureaus in ACYF, including the National Center of Child Abuse and Neglect (NCAN).

4. The authors include a separate section on the evolution of Child Protective Services. Advocates concerned about battered children worked for many years before CAPTA was enacted in 1974. This program created a formal reporting mechanism for child abuse and neglect allegations. This legislation provided for a more formal monitoring of the extent of the problem. However, the magnitude of the problem is exemplified by the number of serious injuries and deaths to children known to CPS agencies.

5. Since the 1970's the development of family preservation services (under various program names such as Homebuilders) has been a major activity within the child welfare system, as workers and agencies began to emphasize the "strengths perspective." Child welfare experts argued that out-of-home placements could be reduced through providing intensive family support services.

6. In spite of the new service approaches, the number of cases of child maltreatment continued to climb, and thus the number of children in foster care grew. As foster care rolls grew, policy makers responded with "permanency planning" as the central feature of the Adoption Assistance and Child Welfare Act of 1980.

7. Adoption has always been a component of child welfare services, given the voluntary surrenders of custody by biological parents. The authors describe a number of controversial issues in adoption in the 1980's and 90's, including transracial and transcultural adoptions and the legality or suitability of gay and lesbian adoptive parents.

8. In discussing Head Start, the authors note that fewer than half of eligible children participate. This is a good discussion issue. Among the variety of reasons is the inadequacy of funds.

9. The authors' discussion of emerging issues presents a broader picture of child welfare issues that can be analyzed individually and as they relate to the traditional child welfare programs.

Teaching Suggestions and Exercises for Student Learning

1. There are many single-case studies of child fatalities attributed to failures in the child welfare system. Identify and discuss one of these cases. If there are no recent local cases, unfortunately *Time* and *Newsweek* regularly report such incidents. What can we learn from studies of such cases?

2. If there are resources available, compare formal training of child welfare workers with the formal training of selected military occupational specialties in the US armed forces.

3. Victims of Child Abuse Laws (VOCAL) suggests that there are sometimes "false positives" when child welfare workers investigate complaints of maltreatment? What can we learn from VOCAL? Are their grievances legitimate? Is there a VOCAL type group in your area? How do child welfare agencies and workers respond to such complaints?

4. It is important to help students understand the traditional child welfare programs and how they are connected. Abused and neglected children are, for the most part, referred to public agencies, although the debate over privatization in this area continues. When social workers determine that a child is at risk, the child may be placed in foster care. While the goal of permanency planning is paramount, the reality is much more complicated. If there are students in the class who work in child welfare, the realities can be explored. If not, a child protective services supervisor is often an ideal guest speaker.

5. The authors include many references to newspaper accounts of child welfare cases. The students can be encouraged to look for such reports in the national and local press. Unfortunately, it is likely that there will be this type of supplemental "current events" material.

6. Three major sources of material on child welfare are highly recommended: the annual reports of the Children's Defense Fund, the publications of the Child Welfare League of America, and, of course, the Encyclopedia of Social Work.

7. Examine, as well, what the General Accounting Office (GAO), and the Issue Briefs and Reports from the Congressional Research Service (CRS) say about the issue of child welfare. CRS reports are available through the offices of members of the Senate and the House of Representatives.

8. If the class has little experience in child welfare, brainstorm the type of other social problems that may be connected. As a supplement, develop an "environment of the child protective supervisor" on the blackboard, asking students to think of all of the community social service agencies (including health, mental health, law, courts education, etc) that would be involved in cases.

9. Add Murray Straus' (1994) *Beating the Devil Out of Them: Corporal Punishment in American Families* and discuss the implications Straus brings up regarding the concept of discipline vs. abuse. There are many debate topics in child welfare. An excellent source which explores controversial topics, representing both sides of the argument is Gambrill and Stein's *Controversial Issues in Child Welfare*. It is useful for students to see both sides of each of the issues.

10. Determine whether or not your community has a CASA (Court Appointed Special Advocates). Invite the Executive Director or one of CASA's *guardian ad litem* to speak to your class regarding legal issues that are involved in parental termination, foster care, adoption, etc.

Classroom Discussion Questions

1. The scope of the problem of child fatalities is difficult to determine. The authors note that estimates vary from 1,000-2,000 per year depending on the source. Some of the fatalities are known to child protective service agencies. Why is it so difficult to determine the extent of this problem?

2. What is the relationship between child abuse and neglect and family violence? Should family violence incidents in the presence of children constitute emotional abuse of the child?

3. What do you believe is the relationship between spanking and child abuse/family violence?

4. Why is the child welfare system so difficult to "fix?"

5. What are some of the issues preventing social workers from entering child welfare agencies?

Spotlight Box

The Children's Bureau (CB) is the oldest federal agency for children and is located within the United States Department of Health and Human Services' Administration for Children and Families, Administration on Children, Youth and Families. It is responsible for assisting States in the delivery of child welfare services - services designed to protect children and strengthen families. The agency provides grants to States, Tribes and communities to operate a range of child welfare services including child protective services (child abuse and neglect) family preservation and support, foster care, adoption and independent living. In addition, the agency makes major investments in staff training, technology and innovative programs. To learn more about this federal agency, go to its website at http://www.acf.hhs.gov/programs/cb.

Chapter 16   Housing Policies

Chapter Overview

This chapter provides an overview of US housing legislation. From the Housing Act of 1937 to present-day HUD and Farmers Home Administration programs, this chapter highlights key aspects of housing legislation as they relate to the homeless, TANF families, and the working poor. Linkages between housing and the need for social services are made. Concepts such as red-lining and urban renewal are explained within the context of authorizing legislation. Current trends in US housing, including homeowner demographics and geographical migration data are provided. Special attention is focused on the special characteristics and needs of the homeless. Suggestions for the reform of housing policy are made.

Learning Objectives

1. The U. S. did not have a national housing policy prior to the Housing Act of 1937. The past four decades of housing policy could be characterized as a mixture of governmental and non-profit initiatives. Much of the innovation in housing policy has originated in the non-profit sector.

2. Red-lining by mortgage lenders is not only an example of racism but also reflects bad business practices. Social workers have a responsibility to educate lenders and monitor their adherence to the letter and the spirit of the Home Mortgage Disclosure Act (1976) and the Community Reinvestment Act (1977).

3. By allowing states to design and administer their own housing programs the Cranston-Gonzalez National Affordable Housing Act (1990) is an example of devolution of federal policy. With state legislators and administrators taking the policy lead social workers may have easier access to decision-makers for purposes of lobbying for changes in housing policy.

4. The Quality Housing and Work Responsibility Act (1998) is considered to be the housing equivalent of the PRWORA.

5. The US spends less on housing assistance than any other western industrial democracy, despite the fact that housing is often the single largest expenditure in a family or individual's household budget.

6. The non-poor population benefits more from housing subsidies than do individuals and families below or at poverty level. The profession must intervene with legislators and housing officials to steer subsidy resources to populations that are most at-risk of living in inadequate housing.

7. Because of distance and isolation factors rural low-income housing needs can be overlooked by housing advocates in their lobbying efforts to secure additional resources.

8. There are severe shortages of affordable unsubsidized housing units available to low-income individuals and family households. Urban re-development initiatives can reduce the availability of housing stock for the poor thus forcing families and individuals to re-locate. Oftentimes a re-location translates into reliance upon emergency housing resources for a period of time.

9. The true extent of homelessness is not known, with national estimates ranging from 280,000 to 3.5 million. What is known are that families (with children) are becoming more prevalent at emergency shelters. Social workers must re-think intervention strategies relative to enhancing the governmental and non-profit sector response to the needs of homeless families.

10. Initiatives for housing reform are discussed in detail toward the end of the chapter and provide information and insight into the enormity of the problem.

Teaching Suggestions and Exercises for Student Learning

1. The "housing" issue is really an issue concerning many agencies and many services. It has become an issue of poverty, homelessness, physical abuse, runaways, mental illness and addiction. Where one chooses to intervene as a social worker then becomes more problematic as policies are seen as being interdependent.

2. Select a geographic area to survey. Depending on circumstances, the area chosen could be a section of a rural or suburban county or neighborhoods in a larger municipality. Using housing as the common theme interview administrators (and clients if permitted) of housing authorities, emergency and family shelters, food banks, street clinics, and church leaders in the area. Ask questions about the availability and desirability of present housing stock and rental units for their clients. Ask about regulations/policies that hinder or help their clientele to obtain housing. Ask what they would like to see changed in terms of housing policy/programs. After the interviews have been completed come together and have the students tell their experiences. Their stories will bring to life the complexities of policy change in the real world of agencies and clients.

3. From this "social experiment," discuss concrete ways to improve policy. Your next class can work on a social action piece to complement and solve for the information you are able to find.

4. Contact your local (or state) housing planning authority and ask for a copy of the latest housing plan. Be sure to inquire about how the agency performed the needs assessment. From what you know of your community or state, is the plan adequate? What parts of the state or which population is still underserved? Will you be participating in the next round of planning? What will you have to do to prepare in terms of information gathering and/or organizing for the next planning session?

5. Visit an emergency shelter. Simply look at the faces of the children. Think about what they are missing in school, who their friends might be, where they slept last night, etc. Where will they sleep next week? Just before a cold spell strikes, take a ride with the outreach team as they try to convince people they find in alleys and under bridges to come into the shelter that night. Share these experiences with your colleagues, with administrators, and with law makers at state and local levels of government. See your experiences translated into policy.

6. The Home Mortgage Disclosure Act (1976) and the Community Reinvestment Act (1977) both tried to rid the lending industry of a practice called "red-lining." How could you find out if local banks and savings and loans continue to "redline" mortgages? Relate "red-lining" to the concept of institutional racism. How would you defend these Acts against the charge that the federal government is attempting 'social engineering'?

7. How would you go about finding the local availability and occupancy rates of single room occupancy (SRO) housing units? Who lives in these housing units? Are the occupants in need of services other than housing?

8. Discuss the common belief that homelessness is a manifestation of poverty. Talk about possible immediate and then long term interventions in light of the discussions you have.

9. The homeless population is often undercounted in federal surveys for political reasons. What would be the political gain for undercounting this population? Discuss your answer in terms of the concepts of empowerment and marginalization of people. Do you see any role for social work?

10. "Think Global-Act Local"-in terms of housing, what implications does this phrase have for you? How can you make a difference?

Classroom Discussion Questions

1. Affordable and safe housing is a need that everyone has, yet government assistance for housing has never been considered an "entitlement" to households that qualify. Discuss this in terms of ethics relative to the idea of housing being a "right" or "core good."

2. The US had no national housing policy prior to the Housing Act of 1937. Discuss the reasons why no housing policy existed. What effect did the Great Depression have on the passing of this legislation?

3. The Housing Acts of 1949 and 1954, the Model Cities Act (1966), and the Housing and Community Development Act (1974) all displaced poor families in the name of urban renewal. Discuss current local urban renewal/development projects in your area. Who do these projects displace? Where do these people re-locate?

4. The Quality Housing and Work Responsibility Act (1998) ties workforce participation to housing benefits. Is this fair?

5. Not only does the federal government fail to adequately support the poor but most housing subsidies benefit the non-poor (through mortgage and property tax income tax deductions). Discuss this in terms of Titmuss' three spheres of welfare. Discuss the influences and political power that supports this subsidy imbalance between the haves and the have-nots.

Spotlight Box

The Office of Community Planning and Development (CPD) seeks to develop viable communities by promoting integrated approaches that provide decent housing, a suitable living environment, and expand economic opportunities for low and moderate income persons. The primary means towards this end is the development of partnerships among all levels of government and the private sector, including for-profit and non-profit organizations.

Consistent with these objectives, the Office of Community Planning and Development has developed a set of underlying principles that are used in carrying out its mission. These principles are: 1. Community building begins with job creation, employment, and creation of safe, decent and affordable housing; 2. Planning and execution of community development initiatives must be bottom up and community driven; 3. Complex problems require coordinated, comprehensive, and sustainable solutions; 4. Government must be streamlined to be made more efficient and effective; 5. Citizen participation in Federal, State and local government can be increased through communication and better access to information.

For more information, visit CPD's website at: www.hud.gov/offices/cpd/index.cfm.

Chapter 17

The Politics of Food Policy and Rural Life

Chapter Overview

This chapter discusses the policies of food production and distribution. The regulations of current government programs such as Food Stamps, WIC (Special Supplemental Nutrition Program for Women, Infants, and Children), and a range of school and community-based nutrition programs are described. The *Face of Hunger* section provides demographics regarding the extent of hunger and food insecurity in the United States. Family and corporate farms in terms of both historical and contemporary economic issues are discussed, as are current social concerns surrounding agricultural laborers.

Learning Objectives

1. Social workers look at the whole person for purposes of assessment and developing intervention strategies. Being aware of the role that inadequate food energy may play in the physical and emotional health of a client is very important. Special attention should be paid to the nutritional intake of children when assessing learning-related issues.

2. Hunger (4% of all US households) and food insecurity (33 million Americans) are continuing issues. The US experiences twice the rate of food insecurity of any other industrial nations in the world.

3. Hunger-relief agencies have found that the greatest increase in hunger has been among the working poor. Social workers must not allow the presence of family income to mask food insecurity of client families.

4. Providing the poor with access to food is a redistributive function of the welfare state. The obligation of the government to provide food to the poor is similar to that of providing economic opportunity. Social workers must continue to work towards the creation of a higher and broader economic safety net for those people at or below the poverty line.

5. Approximately 23 million people participated in the Food Stamps program in 2004, at a cost of $26.4 billion.

6. Almost 70% of food stamp households are single female-headed; this phenomena is known as the feminization of poverty.

7. Public policy regarding food distribution can be paradoxical. WIC, enacted in 1972, is a discretionary program and only half who qualify receive benefits. Yet, the US feeds much of the world with its agricultural excess, meaning that many of its own citizens go hungry.

8. A GAO report found that even though FS and welfare caseloads have declined, the need for food assistance has not diminished.

9. The farming industry in the US has suffered greatly in the past twenty years. In 1981, the total asset value of US agriculture was $1 trillion; by 1985 it had shrunk to $692 billion. Despite hefty price tags for the US government in relation to farm subsidies, farming is still facing the greatest decline of any occupation in America.

10. Sixty one percent of farming families live at or below the poverty line. Income, housing, education, and health care are issues that concern these families.

11. US family farms are quickly being replaced by corporate farms, leading to closed markets where prices are fixed not by open, competitive bidding, but by negotiated contracts.

12. Other issues facing the farming industry that are discussed in Chapter 17 include: genetic engineering, global trade, mad cow disease, local selling, organic farming, global warming, and sustainable agriculture.

Teaching Suggestions and Exercises for Student Learning

1. It is vitally important for students to have an understanding of governmental and community-based food programs as undoubtedly hunger touches many of their clients. Bring in to class local agency/church officials that administer food programs. Have these representatives discuss eligibility requirements and operational concerns of their programs.

2. Concepts and programs discussed in class can come to life and become richer when they are experienced up close and personal. As an assignment have your students visit, or better yet, volunteer time at a local food bank or a community action program that distributes food to helping agencies. Have the students share with the class what they saw and experienced.

3. Ethnocentric thinking can be an obstacle for the creation of innovative policy recommendations. Use Internet technology to explore the domestic food distribution policies of countries that currently export a percentage of their production excess. Discuss these policies in terms of collective or national values.

4. Seasonal agricultural workers are often an invisible population in the host community. It is all too easy to overlook the service needs of these families. Assign students to seek out local agencies/churches that have historically assisted this population and find out the nature of the unmet needs. Use this opportunity to talk about how food distribution policy /programs impact on this fragile population.

5. Discuss why all government food programs are not entitlement programs.

6. The U.S. Conference of Mayors reports that 37 percent of people requesting emergency food assistance in American cities are employed. A Wisconsin study found that one-third of former welfare recipients had problems paying for food despite a high incidence of employment. What do these studies suggest in terms of potential policy changes? Going beyond suggestions for changes in food distribution policy, are there any other areas of policy that would require change to obtain your desired result?

7. From what you know about the Food Stamp program, suggest change(s) you would make in the eligibility and resource regulations? Explain your reasoning for the proposed change(s).

8. Farmers have received government subsidies for growing, and sometimes not growing, certain crops. Should the government continue to subsidize? Discuss in terms of fairness and equality to other sectors of the American economy.

9. Children in seasonal agricultural laborer families are high health risks because of their exposure to pesticides. A study found a 34 percent rate of chronic health conditions among these children, compared to a much lower national rate. Does the government, or do their employers, have any responsibility for their health care? Who has the responsibility for prevention efforts? Discuss in terms of the response of the social work profession to these long-standing problems.

10. Discuss how food production and distribution may be considered global issues.

Classroom Discussion Questions

1. Define the term 'food insecurity.' Discuss possible effects that food insecurity may have on your present clients.

2. Consider the overwhelming scientific evidence regarding the effects that hunger has on human development and posturing, such as Maslow's hierarchy of need. Discuss what more the social work profession can do to support intervention at all levels of practice to address the hunger issue.

3. What ethical obligation if any, does the United States government have to feed the millions of its starving citizens before exporting its excess food to the rest of the world's hungry population?

4. What does this statistic say about America and its citizens: 33 million are food insecure and around 31% are obese or overweight?

5. What are some common misconceptions regarding the demographics and geographics of those on food stamps?

Spotlight Box

The mission of Farm Aid is to keep family farmers on their land. The organization's goal is to bring together family farmers and citizens to restore family farm-centered agriculture. Farm Aid accomplishes this mission by:
  - Raising awareness and funds with an annual signature music concert
  - Awarding grants to farmer and rural service organizations that directly support family farmers
  - Developing an dfunding programs that promote outreach, education, and the development of long-term solutions that support family farm centered agriculture
  - Building partnerships and educating the public to raise funds and to promote activism in support of family farmers

Chapter 18

The American Welfare State
In International Perspective

Chapter Overview

This final chapter looks at the American welfare state in comparison to 174 other nations. The authors provide information regarding how comparisons are made, different typologies of welfare states around the world, and end the last chapter of this book with outlook and predictions for the future. The chapter reports on international aid, or redistribution of wealth from advanced to developing nations. The chapter closes with a report on trends in globalization with information about the International Monetary Fund (IMF), World Bank, General Agreement on Tariffs and Trade (GATT), the World Trade Organization (WTO), and the importance of nongovernmental organizations (NGO's) in facilitating development.

Learning Objectives

1. It is important to understand the individual and residual perspectives. More of the western industrial nations have created welfare states that are regarded as institutional. They provide universal services—or services to all citizens—such as family and/or children's allowances. For upper-income families who do not need such help, the tax system works to balance the subsidy. For lower-income families who need the subsidy, an income floor is provided. The end result is a smaller percent of children who are poor.

2. The U. S. has been called a "reluctant welfare state," using a "safety net" or residual approach that targets some services to the poor alone. Some analysts argue that services for the poor become **poor** services because they have limited political support and are subject to anti-tax sentiment. The end result is higher rates of poverty, particularly among children, minorities, and female-headed families.

3. The typology developed by Gosta Esping-Andersen classifies welfare states as: corporatist, liberal welfare states, and social democratic states. Students may have difficulty sorting out these various refinements; they should remember that these are conceptualizations not standard definitions with fixed criteria. It may be useful to stress the more long-standing conceptualizations_–RESIDUAL V. INSTITUIONAL; UNIVERSAL V, SELECTIVE; Programs for all citizens v. programs and services for the poor alone.

4. Theda Skocpol's notion of "welfare exceptionalism" is another variation on the idea that the US is a "reluctant welfare state." It provides yet another opportunity to ask: Why are we different?

5. The authors note that many of these ideas can be critiqued. The role of the private sector and tax expenditures produces benefits for many citizens that exceed benefits of other countries. The authors note, "...although the United States may lag behind in public welfare provision, people enjoy exceptionally high standards of living...and the country remains a magnet for immigrants from all over the world...."

6. The ranking of national development is a challenging task. The Estes Weighted Index of Social Progress provides an interesting sensitizing theory, but ranking the US 27th in the world is arguable. Estes employs comprehensive criteria, but some assumptions can be challenged.

7. The U. N. Human Development Index (HDI) is based on a composite of three variables: life expectancy, educational attainment, and per capita GDP. The US ranks highly on all criteria and thus is tied in rank for second.

8. Amartya Sen's (Nobel Prize in Economics, 1998) "capability poverty" thesis calls attention to the importance of personal freedom and gives hope for improving social welfare around the world.

9. Table 18.3 illustrates trends in International Aid. Note that while the US makes large dollar amount contributions, in terms of per capita GDP, they are very small.

Teaching Suggestions and Exercises for Student Learning

1. Have your class develop a list of strengths and weaknesses in regard to the US welfare state in international perspective.

2. Have students locate the expenditures on public benefits by other industrialized countries. Encourage students to compare the benefits of increasing or decreasing spending in the US.

3. Utilizing the Human Development Index in Chapter 18, have students compare the US with other countries. Have students discuss whether or not they agree with the criteria for this ranking.

4. Have the class discuss their opinion regarding the involvement of the US in international versus domestic affairs. How much of a "corporate neighbor" should the US be?

5. Often times, subjects on this level are considered by many practitioners to be "too macro." Encourage students to determine how the concepts addressed in Chapter 18 directly apply to Social Work practitioners, regardless of their practice areas or fields.

6. Have your class discuss a current event in which the US is offering foreign aid (as of this press time, two issues are tsunami relief and the rebuilding of Iraq). What is the general feeling of the class regarding these types of efforts? Is there a differentiation?

7. There are other accounts of the impact of globalization that are compelling. Thomas Friedman's (1999) *The Lexxus and the Olive Tree* has been on the New York Times best seller list as both hardback and paperback. Friedman describes the evolution toward a single global market and the democratization of technology, finance, employment, and information. Lester Thurow's *The Future of Capitalism* explores similar themes.

8. Depending on the size and abilities of your class, organize a class project with a local chapter of Habitat for Humanity.

9. Assign the reading of Robert Klitgaard's *Tropical Gangsters*. Discuss infrastructure deficiencies pointed out in the book and how these could relate to the US or other oil-producing/oil-seeking countries.

10. Encourage the class to develop a list of pros and cons regarding the dismissing of debt by the US to developing countries.

Classroom Discussion Questions

1. How is globalization reminiscent of these two expressions: "like painting a moving train" and "overcome by events" (OBE)?

2. Discuss ways in which the three-part classification of nations is useful, but evolving (example: the "Four Tigers" and emergence of the Fourth World.)

3. How do you believe that the US is perceived internationally in regard to the current state of its welfare policy?

4. To what extent is the US free market economic system a factor in international comparisons of welfare states?

5. What are the advantages and disadvantages of capitalism, socialism, communism, and globalization?

Spotlight Box

The International Monetary Fund (IMF) was established by international treaty in 1945 to help promote the health of the world economy. Headquartered in Washington, D.C., it is governed by a global membership of 184 countries.

The IMF is the *central institution* of the international monetary system—the system of international payments and exchange rates among national currencies that enables business to take place between countries.

It aims to **prevent crises** in the system by encouraging countries to adopt sound economic policies; it is also—as its name suggests—*a fund* that can be tapped by members needing temporary financing to address balance of payments problems.

The IMF works for global prosperity by promoting
- the balanced expansion of world trade,
- stability of exchange rates,
- avoidance of competitive devaluations, and
- orderly correction of balance of payment problems

For more information about IMF, visit their website at www.imf.org

---

Test Bank

Chapter 1   Social Policy and the American Welfare State

1) The American Social Welfare system

    A) is a function of the pluralism of American culture.

    B) more influenced by democracy.

    C) more influenced by capitalism.

    D) similar to that of other industrial nations.

Answer: A
Page Ref: 2
Topic: Conceptual

2) American social welfare programs are

    A) in transition.   B) relatively static.

    C) a model for the rest of the world.   D) helpful only for the poor and elderly.

Answer: A
Page Ref: 2
Topic: Applied

3) American social welfare programs are

    A) provided by public and private sectors.   B) exclusively governmental.

    C) solely delivered in the nonprofit sector.   D) regulated primarily by states.

Answer: A
Page Ref: 2
Topic: Factual

4) The function of social welfare is

    A) to help the poor and the nonpoor.

    B) to provide benefits to people to meet basic life needs.

    C) to enhance relationships among people.

    D) all of the above.

Answer: D
Page Ref: 3
Topic: Conceptual

5) Social welfare policy is

    A) usually based a rational set of assumptions and reliable research.

    B) shaped by many values.

    C) rarely a "zero-sum" game.

    D) exemplary in America.

Answer: B
Page Ref: 3
Topic: Conceptual

6) Social welfare is

    A) a subsidy for employers.

    B) mostly an expression of altruism.

    C) never used for social control.

    D) unilaterally governed by the private sector.

Answer: A
Page Ref: 4
Topic: Conceptual

7) American social welfare is

    A) influenced by political and economic factors.

    B) primarily influenced by socialist ideals.

    C) not influenced by the "free market."

    D) primarily an expression of social altruism.

Answer: A
Page Ref: 4
Topic: Conceptual

8) The American economic continuum is

    A) essentially a mixed welfare economy.   B) basically Keynesian in nature.

    C) primarily conservative and free market.   D) primarily liberal in nature.

Answer: A
Page Ref: 6
Topic: Conceptual

9) Socialists see social problems as

    A) a logical consequence of an unjust society.

    B) unavoidable and unresolvable.

    C) a by-product of democracy.

    D) resolvable through government force.

Answer: A
Page Ref: 10
Topic: Conceptual

10) American liberals

    A) established the welfare state.

    B) no longer influence policy.

    C) had little influence on the New Deal.

    D) see social problems as a by-product of democracy.

Answer: A
Page Ref: 11
Topic: Conceptual

11) The Greens/Green Party

    A) promotes social justice and grassroots democracy.

    B) concentrates on environmental issues.

    C) is considered part of the conservative movement.

    D) established the welfare state in 1935.

Answer: A
Page Ref: 13
Topic: Applied

12) Communitarians are

    A) civic republicans.

    B) similar to American Communists.

    C) opposed to European-style social welfare programs.

    D) in favor of community-based welfare.

Answer: A
Page Ref: 13
Topic: Factual

13) Traditional Conservatives

    A) favor lower taxes and less governmental spending.

    B) usually are anti-union.

    C) oppose extending civil rights legislation.

    D) all of the above.

Answer: D
Page Ref: 15
Topic: Factual

14) Libertarians support

    A) very limited government.

    B) strong local government.

    C) strong national government.

    D) welfare reform charged by federal government.

Answer: A
Page Ref: 18
Topic: Factual

15) Neoconservative think tanks

    A) oppose welfare programs.   B) support welfare reform.

    C) support traditional values.   D) all of the above.

Answer: D
Page Ref: 19
Topic: Factual

16) During the last 30 years, the number of human service corporations-for-profit firms providing social welfare through the marketplace has increased dramatically.

Answer: TRUE
Page Ref: 2
Topic: Factual

17) Social welfare policy regulates the provision of benefits to meet peoples' basic life needs, such as food, housing, and health care.

Answer: TRUE
Page Ref: 3
Topic: Factual

18) The relationship between social problems and social welfare policy is linear.

Answer: FALSE
Page Ref: 3
Topic: Conceptual

19) Social policy and its components do not influence the practice of social work; social work is an altruistic profession.

Answer: FALSE
Page Ref: 5
Topic: Conceptual

20) The current "War on Terror" is an example of social welfare policy coming to the forefront of our nations' consciousness, eclipsing the need for one's personal security.

Answer: FALSE
Page Ref: 5
Topic: Applied

21) Like political rights, economic rights are also mandated by the U.S. Constitution.

Answer: FALSE
Page Ref: 6
Topic: Factual

22) The U.S. operates on a democratic capitalism political economy.

Answer: TRUE
Page Ref: 6
Topic: Factual

23) By 2004, the federal budget deficit had reached a record $450 billion.

Answer: TRUE
Page Ref: 9
Topic: Factual

24) By 1980, social welfare accounted for a mere 5% of all federal expenditures.

Answer: FALSE
Page Ref: 11
Topic: Factual

25) Communitarians and civic republicans have political ideologies that are entirely opposite ends of the political spectrum.

Answer: FALSE
Page Ref: 13
Topic: Conceptual

26) What is meant by the authors' statement, "American social welfare policy is in transition."

Answer: By this statement, the authors are referring to the mix of liberalism and conservatism in social welfare policy. The Social Security Act of 1935 established the welfare state as the charge of the Federal government. The shift to conservatism has left the burden of social welfare to private institutions and faith-based organizations.
Page Ref: 2
Topic: Conceptual

27) How is social welfare becoming, as the text describes, a "big business."

Answer: Human service corporations are going from being predominantly public to for-profit entities. Because it is often less expensive for state and federal government entities to "contract out" to these agencies, they are growing in size, number, and profit margin.
Page Ref: 2
Topic: Conceptual

28) In social welfare policy, what are in-kind benefits? Give three examples of what an in-kind benefit might entail for recipients.

Answer: In-kind benefits are proxies for cash. Examples include food stamps, Medicaid, housing vouchers, WIC, and low-income energy assistance.
Page Ref: 3
Topic: Factual

29) What is involved in the practice of "dumping?"

Answer: Some private health care providers employ the practice of dumping. This involves the abrupt transfer of uninsured patients to public hospitals while they suffer from traumatic injuries. Needless to say, some patients die in the process of being "dumped."
Page Ref: 3
Topic: Factual

30) Discuss how social welfare policy can be considered a mechanism of social control.

Answer: Social welfare policy can enforce social control by meeting the basic needs of the disadvantaged, making them less likely to revolt against those in power, seen as their "caretakers."
Page Ref: 4
Topic: Conceptual

31) How does social welfare policy affect social work practice?

Answer: Social policies dictate how the practice of social work is done, with whom, for whom, for how much, and toward what ends. Students should elaborate on each of these points to demonstrate their grasp of the indications social welfare policy has on social work practice.

Page Ref: 4
Topic: Conceptual

32) "Zero-sum game" refers to what practice in social welfare policy?

Answer: THis refers to the fact that many social welfare policies are initiated for the good of some at the expense of others.

Page Ref: 5
Topic: Factual

33) Identify and briefly describe the three major schools of economic thought dominating the American economy.

Answer: Students should elaborate on the Keynesian, classical or free market, and democratic socialism ideology.

Page Ref: 7
Topic: Factual

34) How do advocates of liberalism argue for the advancement of the public good?

Answer: By promoting an expanding economy coupled with the growth of universal, non-means-tested social welfare and health programs.

Page Ref: 11
Topic: Conceptual

35) What are the main differences between traditional liberalism and neoliberalism?

Answer: Neoliberalism is more cautious of government, less antagonistic toward big business, and more skeptical about the value of universal entitlement.

Page Ref: 12
Topic: Factual

36) Discuss what is meant by "good" and "bad" public spending categories. Give an example of each.

Answer: Former Sec. of Labor, Robert Reich, established the concepts of "good" and "bad" public spending. "Good" spending refers to investments made in human capital, such as expenditures on education and job training. "Bad" spending refers to expenditures on stagnant categories such as welfare and price supports.

Page Ref: 12
Topic: Applied

37) What is the "self-reliance school" and where is it gaining in popularity?

Answer: This economic model maintains that a system which meets the real needs of the people, not a focus on trade and economic expansion, are paramount to economic freedom and more accurately measure the quality of life. This ideology is gaining in popularity in impoverished areas of the U.S. and in developing countries.
Page Ref: 14
Topic: Factual

38) Discuss at least two differences between classical and cultural conservatism.

Answer: The text discusses these two political ideologies in great detail on page 15.
Page Ref: 15
Topic: Factual

39) Discuss the general role that government plays in liberalism, neoliberalism, the Green Party, communitarianism, Self–reliance school, classic conservatism, neoconservatism, cultural conservatism, traditionalism and liberalism.

Answer: This is a very general question, measuring students' breadth of knowledge and grasp of Chapter One content in general. Each ideology presents a different view of how the government should operate and function in society.
Page Ref: 17
Topic: Factual

40) What is the four-fold approach taken by the conservative agenda in the 1980s regarding social welfare policy?

Answer: This approach: 1) end the liberal hegemony in social policy, 2) reroutes public policy through the private sector; 3)curtails costly social programs that lessen profits and restrict companies' global competitiveness; and 4)prohibits the resurgence of social programming.
Page Ref: 17
Topic: Conceptual

Chapter 2 Social Welfare Policy Research: A Framework for Policy Analysis

1) An effective policy framework

    A) examines the economic, political, and social feasibility of a policy.

    B) compares existing, similar policies on level grounding.

    C) provides a system of checks and balances between an organization's mission, goals, and outcome.

    D) all of the above

Answer: D
Page Ref: 26
Topic: Factual

2) One goal of a policy analyst may be to

    A) conduct research.   B) act as a legislative consultant.

    C) advocate for underserved populations.   D) all of the above

Answer: D
Page Ref: 26
Topic: Factual

3) An adequate comparative analysis of health systems in the United States, Canada, and Sweden

    A) is not feasible; it is akin to comparing "apples and oranges."

    B) can be useful for all entities involved

    C) involves inordinate amounts of time, energy, and financial obligation.

    D) need not include multimodal research techniques.

Answer: B
Page Ref: 26
Topic: Factual

4) Social work practice is most clearly affected and influenced by

    A) social policy.   B) public opinion.

    C) private sector economics.   D) none of the above

Answer: A
Page Ref: 26
Topic: Factual

5) Environmental scanning is best defined as

    A) surveying a policy's holistic effectiveness on a certain population.

    B) a method used by the Environmental Protection Agency (EPA) to determine the cost–effectiveness of various pollution control policies.

    C) an agency's becoming aware of changing demographic trends and monitoring legislation to determine their "best practice" for target populations.

    D) pilot–testing programs in various environments to determine an agency's most effective means of implementation.

Answer: C
Page Ref: 26
Topic: Conceptual

6) What is most likely to occur with an unsystematic framework for social policy analysis?

    A) unrealized costs

    B) unintended injury to the policy's target population

    C) positive results

    D) A and B only

Answer: D
Page Ref: 28
Topic: Factual

7) Which of the following is NOT a component of the text's proposed policy framework?

    A) the historical background of a policy

    B) a description of the policy

    C) a projection of future trends for the policy's effectiveness

    D) a description of the problem necessitating the policy

Answer: C
Page Ref: 28
Topic: Factual

8) Understanding the historical antecedents of a policy is important because

    A) continuity requires that the analyst identify historical problems that led to the original policy

    B) it helps to curb the tendency of decision makers to reinvent the wheel

    C) A and B only

    D) A only

Answer: C
Page Ref: 29
Topic: Factual

9) In order to determine whether or not a proposed policy will successfully remedy a social problem, the analyst must

    A) understand the parameters of the problem.

    B) acquaint him/herself with the magnitude of the problem.

    C) determine the population affected by the policy.

    D) all of the above.

Answer: D
Page Ref: 30
Topic: Factual

10) Which of the following serves as the guiding principle for a systematic policy analysis?

    A) a policy's goals   B) funding needed to implement the policy

    C) public opinion or support of the policy   D) bipartisan support for the policy

Answer: A
Page Ref: 31
Topic: Factual

11) "Pay-go financing" is best defined as

    A) initiating a program only after sufficient funding has been realized.

    B) funding programs from federal, as opposed to state revenue taxes.

    C) taking from one program to fund another.

    D) none of the above.

Answer: C
Page Ref: 31
Topic: Applied

12) When determining the administrative feasibility of a policy, the analyst should focus on what two administrative aspects?

    A) funding and allocation

    B) administrative "buy in" and employee participation

    C) nature and extent of outcomes

    D) effectiveness and efficiency

Answer: D
Page Ref: 31
Topic: Factual

13) Publicly financed services are provided primarily on the basis of
    A) the severity of the problem.
    B) public willingness to support the target population.
    C) socio-economic status of the target population.
    D) none of the above

Answer: A
Page Ref: 32
Topic: Factual

14) In policy research, what is the best example of primary research?
    A) conducting a telephone survey of area residents to determine their need of an after-school program in the neighborhood
    B) evaluating census data to determine the magnitude of poverty in an area
    C) interviewing legislators to determine their constituents' desire for the expansion of the Earned Income Tax Credit (EITC)
    D) none of the above

Answer: A
Page Ref: 32
Topic: Applied

15) A careful policy analyst will select a policy that
    A) produces utilitarian benefit.
    B) seeks to solve a wide range of societal problems.
    C) is specific and discrete.
    D) none of the above.

Answer: C
Page Ref: 32
Topic: Applied

16) A policy framework attempts to systematically analyze a social policy or program.

Answer: TRUE
Page Ref: 27
Topic: Factual

17) Policy frameworks reflect the understanding that social policy is context sensitive.

Answer: TRUE
Page Ref: 27
Topic: Factual

18) Effective policy analysis must include the analysis of legitimate, unbiased data.

Answer: TRUE
Page Ref: 27
Topic: Factual

19) Prohibition, enacted in 1919, is an excellent example of effective policy analysis put into practice.

Answer: FALSE
Page Ref: 27
Topic: Conceptual

20) Drug enforcement policies (i.e. The War on Drugs) have resulted in a decrease in illegal drug activity, exhibiting that an effective policy framework was instituted for said policies.

Answer: FALSE
Page Ref: 28
Topic: Conceptual

21) The best policy framework is typically resultant from a linear use of models.

Answer: FALSE
Page Ref: 30
Topic: Conceptual

22) In analyzing a new or existing policy, it is imperative that the analyst remain objective, dismissing opinions regarding that policy held by administrative units.

Answer: FALSE
Page Ref: 31
Topic: Conceptual

23) Given the current political and economic climate, it appears unlikely that new social policy initiatives requiring large revenues will be successful.

Answer: TRUE
Page Ref: 31
Topic: Conceptual

24) Because it involves information that is readily accessible to any person with internet access and a computer, intellectual property rights do not apply to the realm of internet research.

Answer: FALSE
Page Ref: 34
Topic: Factual

25) Despite its reliance on a subjective framework, social policy analysis is largely analytical.

Answer: FALSE
Page Ref: 36
Topic: Conceptual

26) Explain the importance of an effective policy framework.

Answer: Students should produce an answer that is similar to the introduction of the concept at the beginning of the chapter. This answer should include a discussion centered around the policy's political, economic and administrative feasibility.

Page Ref: 26
Topic: Conceptual

27) Discuss the different levels (macro and micro) on which policy analysis frameworks can be used by social work practitioners.

Answer: Answers should expound upon the fact that social work practitioners are affected by policies in their agencies determining with whom they will work, what services they will provide and how long. Additionally, on a macro level, these policies will determine what social workers are legally capable of doing and will also dictate for which services they can receive reimbursement, etc.

Page Ref: 26
Topic: Conceptual

28) Discuss some hidden issues that make a social policy such as mandatory drug testing for all employees a complex analysis.

Answer: See questions that text raises on pg. 2–3
Page Ref: 27
Topic: Applied

29) Discuss four of the eight key elements to a well–designed policy framework.

Answer: Answers should include four of the following: systematic analysis, context sensitivity, objective and legitimate data, explicit analytic method, broad–based effect for target population, consideration of unintended consequences a policy may produce, consideration of contextual alternatives, examination of potential policy impacts, both positive and negative.

Page Ref: 27
Topic: Factual

30) What should an effective policy description include?

Answer: Students' answers should include a discussion of policy expectations and how the policy is expected to work, resources or opportunities the policy is expected to provide (power, cash, economic opportunity, etc.), who will receive coverage, policy implementation, short and long term goals, operational administrative auspices, funding, agencies or organizations with administrative oversight, length of time policy is expected to run, knowledge base of the policy (lit review).

Page Ref: 27
Topic: Factual

31) Why is it imperative for policy analysts to understand the value premise of the policy as well as the underlying assumptions it has?

Answer: Answers should include the consideration of some/all of the following: to understand hidden ideological assumptions of the policy, how the target population is viewed or conceptualized in the policy description, social vision that the policy hopes to accomplish, deviation or perpetuation of the status quo, who benefits from the policy. While this is typically the most difficult task for the policy analyst, determining any hidden agendas or underlying mis/conceptions will assist the analyst in objectively analyzing the policy and its effectiveness.

Page Ref: 30
Topic: Conceptual

32) Should a policy analyst keep in mind the political feasibility of a proposed policy when analyzing it? Why or why not?

Answer: YES! Ensure that students' answers consider the fact that social policy is what guides effective practice...without political feasibility or "buy-in" a policy is doomed to failure and only serves as an ineffective use of time, resources, and energy.

Page Ref: 31
Topic: Conceptual

33) Discuss the pros and cons of "pay-go financing."

Answer: PROS: minimum funding often times necessitates this practice...it is a "real world" solution; without any funding, the probability that a policy will be implemented is slim to none; without any funding at all, it is highly unlikely that a policy will be considered at any time in the future; CONS: thinning out resources means that no policy will be appropriately funded; prohibits full realization of benefits of any programs or policies because non are effectively funded

Page Ref: 31
Topic: Conceptual

34) Why does social policy implementation involve economic and political trade-offs?

Answer: In this answer, students should exhibit their understanding of the following concept: "Even in the best of economic times, fiscal resources are always inadequate to meet the breadth of human need." Politically, it is a well-known construct of our legislative system that compromise is often times the only means by which a policy, or a portion of it, will be implemented.

Page Ref: 32
Topic: Applied

35) Discuss the pros and cons of internet research in conducting an effective policy analysis.

Answer: This information can be found in the section of the chapter concerning Internet research (p. 2-17 - 2-25). Students should include mention of reliability, confidentiality, cost, and the like.

Page Ref: 32
Topic: Conceptual

36) Why is it important for a policy analyst to critically evaluate information or recommendations received from think-tank organizations?

Answer: Often times these organizations exist as proponents of a specific cause or population. Information obtained from these organizations is likely to be biased in favor of their cause or population, making an unbiased analysis difficult, if not impossible. Sole reliance on such information is often problematic.

Page Ref: 32
Topic: Applied

37) Discuss issues a policy analyst must keep in mind when utilizing online journals for policy research. Would you recommend this resource? If yes, in what circumstances. If no, why not?

Answer: Journals, while plentiful, can accrue costly subscription costs. Additionally, full journal text is often times not available. Analysts should seek out articles that are peer-reviewed and recent.

Page Ref: 33
Topic: Applied

38) Discuss ethical areas of concern regarding electronic research and utilizing online participants.

Answer: Answers will vary but should include reference, at minimum, to confidentiality and informed consent issues.

Page Ref: 34
Topic: Applied

39) Describe the pros and cons of internet research in conducting an effective policy analysis.

Answer: Answers will vary, but should include some of the following: PROS: breadth of information, instant accessibility, access to hundreds/thousands research participants CONS: difficult to ascertain validity of a website, complicated issues re: confidentiality and informed consent, etc.

Page Ref: 34
Topic: Applied

40) Describe three resources available to policy researchers online.

Answer: Answers will vary, but may include: online libraries, journals, census data, organizational websites, directories, research results, etc.

Page Ref: 34
Topic: Factual

Chapter 3 Religion and Social Welfare Policy

1) Beginning in 1828, what movement sought to end mail delivery on Sundays?

    A) Temperance movement
        B) New England Sabbatariam campaign

    C) Abolitionists' endeavors
        D) none of the above

Answer: B
Page Ref: 41
Topic: Factual

2) What movement is said to have shown the intricate interweaving of religion and politics?

    A) The Great Awakening
        B) Abolition movement

    C) Suffragist movement
        D) all of the above

Answer: A
Page Ref: 41
Topic: Factual

3) The first important national public health group was the

    A) Christian Women for Maternal Health.
        B) Freedman's Bureau.

    C) U.S. Sanitation Commission.
        D) National Institute of Public Health.

Answer: C
Page Ref: 42
Topic: Factual

4) Following the Civil War, what churches immediately reunited?

    A) Catholic
    B) Presbyterian
    C) Baptist
    D) all of the above

Answer: A
Page Ref: 42
Topic: Factual

5) Of the following, which was a major provider of care to impoverished individuals beginning in the late 1800s?

    A) Social welfare policies
        B) Charity Organization Societies

    C) Daughters of the Republic
        D) none of the above

Answer: B
Page Ref: 45
Topic: Factual

6) Who established Hull House?

    A) Dorthea Dix
        B) Jane Addams

    C) Julie Daigrepont McCuen
        D) Abraham Flexner

Answer: B
Page Ref: 46
Topic: Factual

7) What movement served as a reaction to the perceived heartlessness of American society?

   A) Progressive   B) Temperance

   C) Liberalist   D) Christian Coalition

Answer: A
Page Ref: 47
Topic: Factual

8) What single event marked the high point of Protestant dominance in the 19th and early 20th centuries?

   A) Prohibition   B) Abolition

   C) Taxation without Representation   D) all of the above

Answer: A
Page Ref: 47
Topic: Factual

9) What percentage of religious broadcasting was controlled by conservative and evangelical ministers in 1990?

   A) 10   B) 30   C) 75   D) 90

Answer: D
Page Ref: 49
Topic: Factual

10) What court decision expanded the U.S. Constitution's 1st Amendment to include states?

   A) Plessy v. Ferguson   B) Buchli v. Texas

   C) Cantwell v. Connecticut   D) Presbyterian Church USA v. Illinois

Answer: C
Page Ref: 49
Topic: Factual

11) What president coined the phrase "War on Poverty?"

   A) Johnson   B) Kennedy   C) Nixon   D) Carter

Answer: A
Page Ref: 51
Topic: Factual

12) The "Moral Majority" supported

   A) prayer in school.   B) equal rights for all U.S. citizens.

   C) peace talks in the Soviet Union.   D) all of the above.

Answer: A
Page Ref: 51
Topic: Factual

13) White, mainline Protestants comprised whatpercentof voters in 1972?

    A) 45   B) 10   C) 75   D) 25

Answer: A
Page Ref: 53
Topic: Factual

14) Whatpercentof congregations in the U.S. receive public funds as a result of Charitable Choice funding?

    A) 3   B) 9   C) 15   D) 21

Answer: A
Page Ref: 53
Topic: Factual

15) Which statement regarding faith-based organizations (FBOs) is true?

    A) 2/3 of states have pursued outreach efforts to FBOs.

    B) Less than 1/3 of states proved technical assistance to FBOs.

    C) Fewer than 1/4 of states have modified proposal notification processes.

    D) All of the above.

Answer: D
Page Ref: 53
Topic: Factual

16) American social welfare history has been more strongly influenced by Christianity than by any other world religion.

Answer: TRUE
Page Ref: 39
Topic: Factual

17) Responsibility for social welfare relief was initially considered a federal matter, disinvolving the churches and individuals.

Answer: FALSE
Page Ref: 39
Topic: Conceptual

18) In Colonial America, fewer than 1% of American colonists received help from outside of their social support system.

Answer: TRUE
Page Ref: 40
Topic: Factual

19) The majority of Southern abolitionist converts were male property owners.

Answer: FALSE
Page Ref: 41
Topic: Factual

20) Churches were primarily against assisting soldiers who fought in the Civil War, based on the ideology that war is "sinful."

Answer: FALSE
Page Ref: 41
Topic: Conceptual

21) Lutherans, Episcopalians, and Catholics took a strong denominational stand against slavery in the early 1860s.

Answer: FALSE
Page Ref: 41
Topic: Factual

22) In the 1920s, community solidarity became the norm, creating an increase in the number of Protestant denominations.

Answer: FALSE
Page Ref: 43
Topic: Factual

23) Social Darwinists argued for the Federal Government's assistance for society's poor.

Answer: FALSE
Page Ref: 43
Topic: Conceptual

24) The major emphasis of the early social worker was more often on spiritual guidance than material aid.

Answer: TRUE
Page Ref: 44
Topic: Conceptual

25) No special protective legislation for women existed until the early 1900s.

Answer: TRUE
Page Ref: 45
Topic: Factual

26) What is meant by "the Protestant work ethic?"

Answer: This refers to the pervasive Colonial American ideology that those who were able–bodied and yet unemployed were sinners, thereby reinforcing the value of "hard work."
Page Ref: 40
Topic: Conceptual

27) What is thought to be the main result of the 1801 Cane Ridge Camp meeting?

Answer: This meeting is often viewed as the beginning of the second Great Awakening, lending creedance and giving support to the abolitionist movement.
Page Ref: 40
Topic: Conceptual

28) What were the three end-products of the 2nd Great Awakening?

Answer: First, the religious impulse for reform was channeled into private organizations attempting to promote change. Second, female leaders became trained and mobilized to promote this change and lastly, African-American religious leaders began to emerge to lead the AA converts.
Page Ref: 41
Topic: Applied

29) What consideration prompted the creation of the Bureau of Refugees, Freedman, and Abandoned Lands? What was this entity created to do?

Answer: By the close of the Civil War, political leaders realized that emancipation of the slaves without social services and assistance would create a large social problem. The Freedman's Bureau, as it is more commonly known, was created to provide temporary relief for the duration of the war and one year afterward in the areas of emergency rations, employment training and assistance, education, health care, etc.
Page Ref: 42
Topic: Factual

30) How did applying Charles d theory of evolution lead to a problematic set of assumptions regarding economics and sociology?

Answer: Social Darwinism appeared as a result of Darwin's theories and an in-depth discussion of how these theories affected society and the economic models of the time is included on page 43 in the text.
Page Ref: 43
Topic: Conceptual

31) What is meant by the term "the worthy poor?"

Answer: This referred to the concept that poverty was related to laziness, sinful practices, and overall disrespect for the laws of God. Those deemed "worthy poor" were primarily those that had no choice in the matter of being poor: children and widows.
Page Ref: 43
Topic: Conceptual

32) What was the premise on which the Social Gospel movement emerged?

Answer: Social Gospelists believed that industrialization and the "excesses" of capitalism were to blame for many of society's problems. This movement took on social justice and poverty, claiming that the Church had a moral obligation to fight for the rights of the worker.
Page Ref: 44
Topic: Factual

33) Have the values and ethics of the social work profession evolved since its inception? In what ways.

Answer: Yes. The major emphasis of early social workers was on spiritual guidance, rather than material aid.
Page Ref: 44
Topic: Applied

34) How could Charity Organization Societies' goals be considered a means of social control?

Answer: "Friendly visitors," often members of the upper and middle classes, were often called upon to intervene in the lives of the poor and make judgements as to what would and wouldn't be prudent for them. Their often moral superiority complex was viewed by some as a form of social control..."we'll give you what you need if you do X, Y, & Z."
Page Ref: 45
Topic: Conceptual

35) Compare and contrast Charity Organization Societies and settlement houses.

Answer: Settlement houses were more akin to modern-day social work practice than COS. They were entities established within the neighborhoods they served and they sought to help people in these neighborhoods mobilize themselves for action. Settlement houses were thought to be less patronizing forms of charity.
Page Ref: 46
Topic: Applied

36) What did Abraham Flexner find regarding the profession of social work?

Answer: Flexner judged that Social Work lacked "all the requirements of a profession, particularly a scientifically derived knowledge base that was transmittable."
Page Ref: 46
Topic: Conceptual

37) Discuss how "new media" affected religious groups and the dissemination of their agendas.

Answer: The infiltration of television and radio into American society allowed for religious groups to reach widespread audiences, somewhat commercializing religion.
Page Ref: 49
Topic: Applied

38) What does the term "Charitable Choice" refer to and for what does it allow?

Answer: This provision is fully discussed, along with implications of its implementation on page 53 in the text.
Page Ref: 53
Topic: Applied

39) Why is it unlikely that faith-based organizations have the capacity and commitment to sustain comprehensive and long-term services?

Answer: Possible answers to this question are included on page 54 in the text.
Page Ref: 54
Topic: Conceptual

40) What does the Chavez National Congregations Study indicate?

Answer: This study indicates that congregation-based social services are advanced by the smallest handful of volunteers, and that social services on a more widespread basis would be overwhelming. It indicates that no qualitative or quantitative data suggests the superiority of effectiveness of congregations vs. government entities.

Page Ref: 54
Topic: Conceptual

Chapter 4   Discrimination in American Society

1) According to the text, economic, social and political discrimination often leads to poverty, which in turn, results in the need for

   A) social programs.

   B) legislative action.

   C) an examination of American political priorities.

   D) widespread income re–distribution.

   Answer: A
   Page Ref: 59
   Topic: Factual

2) The "frustration–aggression hypothesis" maintains that discrimination is a form of aggression activated

   A) when society becomes frustrated with economic policies.

   B) when an individual's needs become frustrated.

   C) by individuals with a psychiatric proclivity toward antisocial personality disorder.

   D) when rage is passively expressed.

   Answer: B
   Page Ref: 59
   Topic: Factual

3) That individuals hold prejudicial attitudes because of their socialization is an example of

   A) a Marxian explanation of prejudice.

   B) a discounted theory.

   C) the normative–cultural explanation of prejudice.

   D) the frustration–aggression hypothesis of discrimination.

   Answer: C
   Page Ref: 59
   Topic: Applied

4) Of the reasons listed below, what does the text purport as being necessary for discriminatory practices to appear valid?

   A) strong leadership capable of perpetuating discriminatory thoughts and beliefs

   B) social legitimation

   C) historical validity

   D) none of the above

   Answer: B
   Page Ref: 60
   Topic: Factual

5) According to the U.S. Census Bureau, minority groups will no longer be a "true minority" around the year

   A) 2030.

   B) 2040.

   C) 2050.

   D) The U.S. Census Bureau does not make any such assumptions regarding minority populations.

   Answer: C
   Page Ref: 61
   Topic: Factual

6) Which group below constitutes the fastest growing Spanish–speaking subgroup in the U. S.?

   A) Puerto Ricans   B) Cuban Americans

   C) Mexican Americans   D) Spanish Americans

   Answer: C
   Page Ref: 68
   Topic: Factual

7) Which of the following statements is NOT true of the American Indian populations?

   A) American Indian were granted citizenship in 1924.

   B) There is no single definition of an American Indian.

   C) American Indians have a maternal death rate lower than the national average.

   D) Housing and education remain major problems to the American Indian population.

   Answer: C
   Page Ref: 70
   Topic: Conceptual

8) What is the most comprehensive welfare reform legislation since the New Deal to affect legal and illegal immigration in the United States?

   A) Personal Responsibility and Work Opportunity Reconciliation Act (PRWORA)

   B) USA Patriot Act

   C) Immigration and Naturalization Services (INS) Borders Act

   D) Enhanced Border Security Act

   Answer: A
   Page Ref: 74
   Topic: Factual

9) VAWA is

    A) a law that reflects a comprehensive approach to domestic violence.

    B) designed to improve the response of police and prosecutors to crimes of sexual assault.

    C) a vehicle to enforce protection orders.

    D) all of the above.

Answer: D
Page Ref: 76
Topic: Factual

10) Regarding same sex relationships which statement below is NOT accurate?

    A) DOMA was passed in part as a reaction to court decisions in the state of Hawaii.

    B) Many municipalities across the U.S. have passed legislation extending benefits to partners of city employees.

    C) Because of equal protection laws, sexual orientation can no longer be considered a factor in child custody disputes.

    D) Vermont recognizes same–sex unions.

Answer: C
Page Ref: 77
Topic: Factual

11) The wage gap between women and men in the U.S. is

    A) shrinking slowly.

    B) non–existent.

    C) expanding slowly due to states striking down affirmative action legislation.

    D) rapidly closing.

Answer: A
Page Ref: 79
Topic: Conceptual

12) Which of the following statements regarding our nation's elder population is NOT accurate?

    A) Elders represent 13% of the U.S. population, receiving over 60% of federal spending expenditures.

    B) A full 10% of elderly live below the poverty line.

    C) 85% of elderly persons are white individuals.

    D) Approximately 60% of those over the age of 85 live in nursing homes.

Answer: D
Page Ref: 81
Topic: Factual

13) Which statement below is NOT accurate?

    A) Title XX Social Services Block Grant is the largest federal program for child care services.

    B) Most industrialized nations, except the U.S., provide a tax-free family allowance ranging from $300–$600 yearly.

    C) The Family and Medical Leave Act allows for limited paid maternity leave.

    D) The availability of day care has increased rapidly in terms of the number of vacancies and the number of day care centers.

Answer: C
Page Ref: 83
Topic: Factual

14) The Equal Rights Amendment (ERA)

    A) would have nullified all laws on the basis of gender.

    B) would have affected only public employment.

    C) was ratified by less than half of the state legislatures.

    D) would not have affected property rights of married women.

Answer: B
Page Ref: 84
Topic: Conceptual

15) Gov. Jeb Bush, in signing the One Florida Plan (1999) legislation,

    A) prohibited using racial preferences in university admissions.

    B) implemented state-wide a plan to expand the use of racial preferences in the hiring practices of agencies under his control.

    C) allowed non-profit agencies to hire on the basis of race.

    D) abolished affirmative action in that state.

Answer: A
Page Ref: 98
Topic: Factual

16) The "frustration–aggression hypothesis" was formulated by Theodore Adorno.

Answer: FALSE
Page Ref: 59
Topic: Factual

17) Those who exhibit "authoritarian personality" often discriminate because they oppose rigidity and conformity toward an authority figure or entity.

Answer: FALSE
Page Ref: 59
Topic: Conceptual

18) The middle-class is a well-defined social stratification class in America.

Answer: FALSE
Page Ref: 61
Topic: Applied

19) After rising in the mid-1990s, the nationwide number of poor African-Americans has dropped dramatically, in part due to revamped social welfare programs.

Answer: FALSE
Page Ref: 64
Topic: Factual

20) In 1997, over 50% of all minority-owned businesses whose sales exceeded one million dollars were Mexican-American owned.

Answer: FALSE
Page Ref: 69
Topic: Factual

21) The U.S. Census Bureau projects that in less than 50 years immigration will cause the population of the United States to increase approximately 40%.

Answer: TRUE
Page Ref: 73
Topic: Factual

22) Although legislation passed after 9/11 has had a profound impact on border controls and immigration policy, the United States continues to increase the number of refugees allowed asylum in our country.

Answer: FALSE
Page Ref: 74
Topic: Factual

23) According to a 2004 AFL-CIO study, three in five working women women reported earning HALF or more of their families' incomes.

Answer: TRUE
Page Ref: 78
Topic: Factual

24) The abortion rate in the United States decreased by 11 percent from 1994-2000, due to educational programs offered by pro-life organizations around the U.S.

Answer: FALSE
Page Ref: 86
Topic: Factual

25) The ADA specifies that employers are only able to discriminate against candidates with disabilities if his/her disability is of a psychiatric nature.

Answer: FALSE
Page Ref: 97
Topic: Conceptual

26) What are common motives for discrimination, as discussed in the text?

Answer: The text categorizes motives into psychological, normative-cultural, and economic reasons. Students should expand on each of these categories as applied in the text.
Page Ref: 59
Topic: Factual

27) How can we, as social workers, combat prejudice expressed through the "normative-cultural" explanation?

Answer: Students should conceptualize that this form of prejudice is explained by an adherence to societal and institutional norms that support discriminatory practices. Answers will vary, but students should show mastery of the fact that a social worker will often work to combat these prejudices through advocacy, education, and direct practice means.
Page Ref: 59
Topic: Applied

28) How would a Marxist explain discriminatory practices?

Answer: A Marxist sees discriminatory practices as being economically useful to the capitalist class. Marginal and unskilled workers are employed by the economically franchised class and must be willing to work according to the needs of this class.
Page Ref: 59
Topic: Applied

29) Discuss how the federal governments accumulation of data contributes to the concept of racism.

Answer: The census divides U.S. society along the lines of white and people with color and does not account for the important cultural differences among different factions of white and colored individuals.
Page Ref: 60
Topic: Conceptual

30) In what ways does racism typically manifest?

Answer: Students should address one or more of the following: hiring and firing, promotions, differential resource allocation in health care and education, differential transportation, segregation in housing, discriminatory practices of judicial and law enforcement agencies, stereotypical medial images.
Page Ref: 61
Topic: Conceptual

31) Describe how "institutional racism" develops.

Answer: Institutional racism is the culmination of years and years of "strongly entrenched" racism in a society. Though it takes many generations to develop, often it is the most difficult racism to recognize and thus, combat.

Page Ref: 61
Topic: Conceptual

32) Discuss at least 3 of the factors contributing to African–Americans being disproportionately represented among impoverished individuals.

Answer: There are several answers students may choose. Reference pages 64 through 68.

Page Ref: 64
Topic: Conceptual

33) Discuss at least two major changes to immigration law since 9/11.

Answer: Students should be able to bring to mind the USA Patriot Act, the Enhanced Border Security Act, and the Homeland Security Act of 2002. You may also find that students desire to discuss the changes made in regard to foreign students and refugees.

Page Ref: 74
Topic: Conceptual

34) Discuss the concept of the feminization of poverty and explain why women tend to be more impoverished than their male counterparts.

Answer: Answers will vary, but each should speak to the complexity of the problem. The term was coined by Diana Peirce in 1978 to explain the women represent an increasingly larger proportion of the economically disadvantaged. Students may mention disproportionate representation of women in low-paying jobs, the high cost of child care, inequities in the public transfer programs, United States' public policy re: single mothers in comparison to European nations, etc.

Page Ref: 76
Topic: Conceptual

35) Discuss three of the barriers named in the text that women face in the workplace to being equal to their male counterparts.

Answer: Students may offer a multitude of answers including, but not limited to: pregnancy, high day care costs, the glass ceiling, health insurance, sexual harassment, and the inflexibility of work schedules.

Page Ref: 83
Topic: Factual

36) Discuss the religious and psychological explanations behind the concept of homophobia.

Answer: Justification for homophobia on a religious stand has been viewed as a "sin against God" and against religious dogma. Psychologically, it is often viewed as a disease or symptom of arrested development or a fear of intimacy with members of the opposite sex.

Page Ref: 91
Topic: Conceptual

37) Discuss at least three ways in which the concept of ageism affects our society.

Answer: Answers will vary. Pages 4-80 through 4-85 discuss a myriad of effects caused by our nations idolization of youth.
Page Ref: 92
Topic: Applied

38) Discuss how the psychosocial model views the concept of "disabled."

Answer: Essentially, a psychosocial approach to disability looks at it as a socially constructed and defined category. Poverty in the disabled is a result of discrimination, not personal inadequacies, as an example.
Page Ref: 94
Topic: Conceptual .

39) How did the passage of the Americans with Disabilities Act affect employment hiring practices?

Answer: Students should be able to discuss that employers are not able to discriminate against a person with a disability, if they are otherwise qualified for the job. Additionally, employers cannot ask a person if they have a disability and may not use screening tests to determine such information. They must provide "reasonable accommodation" to employees with disabilities and all employers with 15 or more employees must comply with the ADA.
Page Ref: 96
Topic: Conceptual

40) Discuss at least three legal attempts made to remedy discrimination in the United States.

Answer: A myriad of answers to this question can be found on pages 4-94 through 4-98.
Page Ref: 97
Topic: Conceptual

Chapter 5 Poverty in America

1) How many millions of Americans were living in poverty in 2003?

    A) 10   B) 36   C) 42   D) 22

Answer: B
Page Ref: 114
Topic: Factual

2) In 2003, the poverty rate among children was

    A) 26.9%.   B) 17.6%.   C) 32.8%.   D) 10.1%.

Answer: B
Page Ref: 114
Topic: Factual

3) From 2002 to 2003, the poverty rate among the aged

    A) increased.   B) was not analyzed.

    C) decreased.   D) stayed the same.

Answer: D
Page Ref: 114
Topic: Factual

4) The largest number of poor Americans are

    A) White.   B) Black.   C) Asian.   D) Hispanic.

Answer: A
Page Ref: 115
Topic: Factual

5) In 2002, the poverty rate among Blacks was

    A) 10.2%.   B) 42.5%.   C) 24.1%.   D) 35.7%.

Answer: C
Page Ref: 115
Topic: Factual

6) In 2002, the poverty rate among Hispanics was

    A) 21.8   B) 45.2   C) 19.8   D) 35.7

Answer: A
Page Ref: 115
Topic: Factual

7) From 1999–2002, the poverty rate among Blacks

    A) fell.   B) was not analyzed.

    C) stayed the same.   D) increased.

Answer: A
Page Ref: 115
Topic: Factual

8) From 1999–2000, the poverty rate among Hispanics

    A) stayed the same.   B) fell.

    C) increased.   D) cannot be measured.

Answer: B
Page Ref: 115
Topic: Factual

9) From 1999–2002, the poverty rate among Whites

    A) decreased.   B) increased.

    C) stayed the same.   D) was equal to that of blacks.

Answer: B
Page Ref: 115
Topic: Factual

10) The current federal minimum wage is

    A) $7.00   B) $4.75   C) $5.95   D) $5.15

Answer: D
Page Ref: 124
Topic: Factual

11) In 2003, how many states had minimum wages above the federally required rate?

    A) 45   B) 20   C) 13   D) none

Answer: C
Page Ref: 125
Topic: Factual

12) The current value of the federal minimum wage as a percent of the 1997 poverty line for a family of 3 is

    A) 103%.   B) 93%.   C) 71%.   D) 83%.

Answer: D
Page Ref: 125
Topic: Factual

13) In 2003, the poverty level for a one-person family was

    A) $8,501.   B) $9,393.   C) $6,472.   D) $10,501.

Answer: B
Page Ref: 125
Topic: Factual

14) In 1999, the poverty level for a three-person family was

    A) $10,419.   B) $7,763.   C) $22,968.   D) $14,680.

Answer: D
Page Ref: 125
Topic: Factual

15) In 2003, the poverty level for a four-person family was

    A) $18,810.   B) $20,241.   C) $28,544.   D) $16,050.

Answer: A
Page Ref: 126
Topic: Factual

16) Culture of poverty theorists maintain that poverty traits are not transmitted intergenerationally, but rather culturally.

Answer: FALSE
Page Ref: 111
Topic: Conceptual

17) Before his ulterior motives were exposed, Hitler's racial and genetic theories increased the popularity of the Eugenics movement.

Answer: FALSE
Page Ref: 112
Topic: Factual

18) Radicals define poverty as the result of exploitation by the ruling or dominant class under capitalism.

Answer: TRUE
Page Ref: 113
Topic: Applied

19) For most Americans experiencing poverty, it is a static process, meaning it usually remains at consistent levels.

Answer: FALSE
Page Ref: 113
Topic: Conceptual

20) "Spells of poverty" are most often ended by family reconstitution.

Answer: TRUE
Page Ref: 113
Topic: Factual

21) The number of persons living below the poverty line has steadily increased every year since 1959.

Answer: FALSE
Page Ref: 115
Topic: Factual

22) According to the Census Bureau, almost 75% of custodial parents received child support in 2002.

Answer: TRUE
Page Ref: 117
Topic: Factual

23) Since 1959, the poverty rate for the elderly has decreased consistently.

Answer: TRUE
Page Ref: 118
Topic: Factual

24) More than one-half of the rural poor live in the Northeast.

Answer: FALSE
Page Ref: 119
Topic: Factual

25) The minimum wage is adjusted annually for cost of living increase.

Answer: FALSE
Page Ref: 124
Topic: Factual

26) What is the difference between absolute and relative poverty? Which is given more focus in contemporary social welfare policy?

Answer: Absolute poverty refers to a base standard of what is necessary for survival. Anyone who falls below this line is considered poor. Relative poverty focuses on the deprivation relative to the standard of living enjoyed by other members of society. Absolute poverty is more commonly considered in our society.
Page Ref: 111
Topic: Applied

27) What type of society enables the Culture of Poverty to flourish?

Answer: Those societies where a cash economy is based on wage labor and production for profit; high rates of under- and unemployment; commonality of low wages; failure to provide social, economic,and political organization for the "underclasses;"and a focus on the accumulation of wealth and upward mobility typically enable the COP to flourish.

Page Ref: 111
Topic: Conceptual

28) Discuss five of the 14 elements indicated in the culture of poverty. How do these contribute to a culture perpetuating poverty?

Answer: These 14 elements are named on page 112 in the text. Common sense links can be made as to how these elements contribute to the cycle of poverty and its culture.

Page Ref: 112
Topic: Applied

29) Discuss how socialists view poverty as a necessity for capitalism.

Answer: Poverty provides capitalists with an army of surplus laborers who can be used to depress the wages of workers, thereby keeping production costs low and profit margins high.

Page Ref: 113
Topic: Applied

30) What are some of the structural problems attributed to the poverty index. Discuss at least three.

Answer: The poverty index is plagued by a variety of structural issues, including counting in-kind benefits when counting family income, the cost of earning income (ie: transportation to and from work, purchasing proper work attire, etc.); disregard for cost of living variations around the nation, ignores the impact of tax payments for individuals, ignores the effects of the EITC, ignores medical costs, it doesn't account for changing consumption patterns and expenses.

Page Ref: 115
Topic: Factual

31) What progress has been made since 1960 in reducing poverty?

Answer: Refer to Table 5.1 for the general numbers, however, student answers will vary in regard to measures taken to reduce poverty.

Page Ref: 115
Topic: Applied

32) How has poverty changed since 1980?

Answer: Answers will vary, but Table 5.1 references figures pertinent to this question. Additionally, students should be able to point to a shift toward conservatism as a factor in the change regarding poverty.

Page Ref: 115
Topic: Applied

33) What is meant by the phrase "the working poor?" Who comprises this group?

Answer: There are several definitions that students may give, but for standard purposes, the working poor are those who spend at least 27 weeks in the labor force per year (working or looking for work), but whose families fall below the poverty line.
Page Ref: 120
Topic: Conceptual

34) What are the three reasons given for the cause of poverty?

Answer: In depth discussion of these reasons is provided on page 120 of the text.
Page Ref: 120
Topic: Factual

35) Why is the unemployment rate considered by many to be a misrepresentation?

Answer: This rate doesn't take into account those who are underemployed or those who are "discouraged workers" and simply give up their search for employment due to the frustration of not being able to find a job.
Page Ref: 121
Topic: Conceptual

36) Discuss the differences in the primary and secondary labor market.

Answer: The primary market offers jobs which possess high wages, good working conditions, employment stability and job security, equity, due process in the administration of work rules and opportunities for advancement within. Secondary labor market workers may be subject to low wages, poor working conditions, considerable variability in employment, harsh and arbitrary discipline and little opportunity for advancement.
Page Ref: 123
Topic: Applied

37) How does poverty vary (by age, sex, education, employment, etc)?

Answer: This question references facts and figures found throughout the chapter. Answers will vary.
Page Ref: 124
Topic: Applied

38) How are Individual Development Accounts (IDAs) designed to affect poverty?

Answer: IDAs are part of an asset–building strategy to enable poor individuals to accumulate assets by setting up savings accounts, matched by private and public resources, to buy land, houses, etc.
Page Ref: 126
Topic: Factual

39) Discuss the three basic strategies for combating poverty.

Answer: 1) CURATIVE: helps the poor to become self-supporting through changes in their personal lives and environment; 2)ALLEVIATIVE: public assistance programs that seek to ease the suffering, rather than remove the problem; and 3)PREVENTATIVE: social insurance program against accidents, sickness, death, etc.
Page Ref: 126
Topic: Applied

40) Discuss at least three mechanisms of credit in the fringe economy?

Answer: Pages 130–136 discuss the different exploitations of the poor through the fringe economy.
Page Ref: 131
Topic: Conceptual

Chapter 6 The Voluntary Sector Today

1) Which of the agencies below would be in the Voluntary Sector

   A) a for- profit child care facility.

   B) a Veterans Administration facility.

   C) a Family Service Association of America agency.

   D) none of the above.

   Answer: C
   Page Ref: 146
   Topic: Conceptual

2) The term "compassionate conservatism" is associated with

   A) the Republican Party.   B) faith-based social services.

   C) the Democratic Party.   D) the New Deal.

   Answer: B
   Page Ref: 146
   Topic: Factual

3) David Stoesz has posited that _____ groups can be identified within American Social Welfare.

   A) 5   B) 4   C) 3   D) 2

   Answer: B
   Page Ref: 146
   Topic: Factual

4) The influence of _____ grew as a result of the Social Security Act of 1935.

   A) clinical entrepreneurs   B) for-profit agencies

   C) welfare bureaucrats   D) traditional providers

   Answer: C
   Page Ref: 146
   Topic: Factual

5) What 1930s event discouraged a unilinear evolution between the federal welfare bureaucrats and traditional providers?

   A) prohibition of federal welfare funds being given to private agencies

   B) discord among the public and private sector

   C) election of President Hoover

   D) all of the above

   Answer: A
   Page Ref: 147
   Topic: Factual

6) According to the National Association of Social Workers, approximately _____ % of their members are in private practice.

   A) 50   B) 30   C) 20   D) 10

Answer: D
Page Ref: 148
Topic: Factual

7) The National Association of Social Workers did not officially sanction privately practicing social workers until

   A) 1983.   B) 1975.   C) 1964.   D) 1991.

Answer: C
Page Ref: 148
Topic: Factual

8) What do authors point to as being the reason that clinical entrepreneurs are not more well-positioned to lobby for social welfare interests?

   A) private interests superceding philanthropic desires

   B) exclusivity of clientele serviced by private practitioners

   C) incursion of managed care

   D) all of the above

Answer: C
Page Ref: 149
Topic: Factual

9) Purchasing social services from private providers was allowed under which Amendment to the Social Security Act?

   A) Title XIX   B) Title XX   C) Section 473   D) Title X

Answer: B
Page Ref: 151
Topic: Factual

10) Which of the following programs did not originate in the voluntary sector?

   A) TANF   B) Title XX   C) food stamps   D) Medicaid

Answer: A
Page Ref: 154
Topic: Conceptual

11) Maintaining a local symphony through the use of the tax code would be an example of what type of philanthropy?

   A) cerebral   B) bourgeois

   C) elite   D) none of the above

Answer: C
Page Ref: 159
Topic: Conceptual

12) Faced with declining revenues, some voluntary sector agencies have experimented with
    A) bourgeois.   B) purchase of service contracts.
    C) commercialism.   D) compassionate conservatism.

    Answer: C
    Page Ref: 160
    Topic: Factual

13) Ben & Jerry's ice-cream company's WALD initiative represents a new trend in the non-profit sector called
    A) commercialism.   B) privatization.
    C) social entrepreneurship.   D) compassionate conservatism.

    Answer: C
    Page Ref: 161
    Topic: Applied

14) Which of the following federal agencies granted the most money to faith-based organizations?
    A) Health and Human Services   B) Labor
    C) Housing and Urban Development   D) Justice

    Answer: A
    Page Ref: 163
    Topic: Conceptual

15) The 9/11 Victim's Compensation Fund dispensed $ _____ to _____ families.
    A) 238 million; 5,000   B) 2 billion; 1,591
    C) 7 billion; 5,000   D) 10 billion; 10,000

    Answer: C
    Page Ref: 164
    Topic: Factual

16) The primary reason for renewed interest in the voluntary sector has been the reluctance of taxpayers and politicians to authorize major new governmental welfare initiatives.

    Answer: TRUE
    Page Ref: 146
    Topic: Conceptual

17) The influence of welfare bureaucrats shrank as a result of the Social Security Act of 1935.

    Answer: FALSE
    Page Ref: 147
    Topic: Factual

18) The Generosity Index suggests that a state's charity is inversely related to its wealth.

    Answer: TRUE
    Page Ref: 150
    Topic: Factual

19) The Democratic party embraced the voluntary sector as a means to address social problems, while limiting governmental spending on these problems.

Answer: FALSE
Page Ref: 151
Topic: Conceptual

20) Title XX allowed for the "purchase of services" from private providers.

Answer: TRUE
Page Ref: 151
Topic: Factual

21) About half of all charitable dollars comes from families with incomes of under $25,000.

Answer: TRUE
Page Ref: 152
Topic: Factual

22) Total charitable giving in 2002 accounted for approximately 15% of the nation's GDP.

Answer: FALSE
Page Ref: 152
Topic: Factual

23) The value of the four George W. Bush tax cuts is estimated at a total $1.9 billion dollars over 10 years.

Answer: FALSE
Page Ref: 153
Topic: Factual

24) The Charitable Giving Act of 2003 received wide acceptance from foundations and thus passed without question in the 2004 legislative session.

Answer: FALSE
Page Ref: 159
Topic: Factual

25) After 9/11, the public's soured attitude toward charitable giving, due to the United Way incident, improved greatly.

Answer: FALSE
Page Ref: 164
Topic: Factual

26) Discuss the four structural interests in the U.S. social welfare system.

Answer: The four structural interests considered in the social welfare system are traditional providers, welfare bureaucrats, clinical entrepreneurs,and human service executives. Discussion of these four entities can be found on pages 147–149 in the text.
Page Ref: 147
Topic: Conceptual

27) What difference do you see as being the most significant between the ideology of human service executives and clinical entrepreneurs?

Answer: The primary difference is that human service executives are salaried, employed persons in institutions and/or firms. They have less autonomy, but more job security, for the most part.
Page Ref: 149
Topic: Conceptual

28) How have members of marginalized groups secured positions within welfare bureaucracies?

Answer: The text points to the assistance of affirmative action, although student opinions and thus answers will vary.
Page Ref: 150
Topic: Applied

29) What did the 1994 Congress establish with their "Contract with America?"

Answer: Congress established arguments for the overhaul of the welfare system, reducing dependency on public assistance and thus empowering individuals with the ability to "make a better life for themselves."
Page Ref: 151
Topic: Factual

30) How has Title XX affected the governmental welfare state?

Answer: Title XX allowed for the purchase of contract services from private providers, establishing the human services industry as primarily a for-profit institution.
Page Ref: 151
Topic: Applied

31) Discuss the effects of 9/11 on charitable giving overall.

Answer: Because 9/11 adversely affected our economy, dampened philanthropic activity overall. From 2001–2002 contributions fell approximately 1.2% and the perceived mismanagement of the $2.6 billion raised for relief efforts decreased confidence in charity giving overall.
Page Ref: 153
Topic: Conceptual

32) What do analysts note as being the reasons for charitable giving decreases during the Reagan presidency, a time when the voluntary sector was heavily depended upon?

Answer: Analysts cite a poor economy, reductions in government assistance, and adverse tax law.
Page Ref: 153
Topic: Conceptual

33) How has the voluntary sector been important to U.S. social welfare.

Answer: It has been the source of efforts to advance the rights of disenfranchised populations in regard to social justice matters.

Page Ref: 153
Topic: Applied

34) John Gardner asserts that the voluntary sector is responsible for "virtually every far-reaching social change in our history." Name at least three of these social changes and discuss their implications for the advancement of social justice.

Answer: "The abolition of slavery, the reforms of populism, child labor laws, the vote for women and minorities, civil rights, and so on," are some of Gardner's examples, however, it is important to note that students may be able to come up with more contemporary issues, as well.

Page Ref: 154
Topic: Applied

35) What is the most commonly-cited reason for a notable decrease in the United Way's funding?

Answer: Financial indiscretions, including inappropriate use of funds and personal use of funds by the organization's leader are commonly cited as the reason for a drop in United Way's funding.

Page Ref: 157
Topic: Conceptual

36) What was the Charitable Giving Act of 2003 and why was it undesirable to foundations?

Answer: The CGA of 2003 required that foundations give 5% of their endowments annually to charities, excluding operational costs. Current law allows foundations to include operational costs in this 5%. This Act was expected to increase gifts by $4.3 billion, however Foundations fought the Act and it died in the House Ways and Means Committee.

Page Ref: 159
Topic: Conceptual

37) To what does the term "elite philanthropy" refer?

Answer: This concept refers to the large monies given by foundations that totals about $13 billion per year, as opposed to "bourgeois philanthropy" which is in reference to the gifts of individuals.

Page Ref: 159
Topic: Factual

38) What reason is cited for the large disparity in salary between non-profit executives and their "field" workers?

Answer: Non profit executives are expected to socialize with for-profit executives and business heads in order to acquire funding for their organizations. To do this, and do it well, salaries must be inordinately large to accommodate social obligations of entertainment, memberships, and the like.

Page Ref: 160
Topic: Factual

39) What is commercialization and how does it serve non-profits?

Answer: Discussion of this concept is found on pages 161-162 in the text.

Page Ref: 161
Topic: Conceptual

40) Describe the Mueller Macaroni Company scandal. What happened as a result of this scandal?

Answer: New York University Law School alumni bought the company in order to run it as a fund-raising entity for the law school. Questions were raised, and the situation became controversial, however, when it was realized that their non-profit status allowed them to avoid taxation, and reduce production costs, thereby resulting in a monopoly of sorts. As a result of this controversy, tax laws were altered, making income from commercial activities not related to the service function of the non-profit taxable.

Page Ref: 161
Topic: Applied

Chapter 7   Privatization and Human Service Corporations

1) Privatization of social welfare is

    A) the private provision of public services.   B) the public provision of private services.

    C) not legal in the United States.   D) none of the above.

Answer: A
Page Ref: 169
Topic: Applied

2) Privatization may include

    A) private provision of government funded services.

    B) selling government assets.

    C) using vouchers.

    D) all of the above.

Answer: D
Page Ref: 169
Topic: Applied

3) The business community influence social welfare in many ways, including all but which one of the following?

    A) promoting social policies such as universal health care

    B) providing benefits to employees

    C) developing services in response to human needs

    D) providing grants through company–sponsored Foundations

Answer: A
Page Ref: 169
Topic: Conceptual

4) John Donahue contends that the U.S. would save how much if 1/4 of welfare services were privatized?

    A) $30 billion

    B) $500 million

    C) $10 billion

    D) Donahue actually asserts that government expenses would rise.

Answer: A
Page Ref: 170
Topic: Factual

5) Privatization of social welfare began to grow in the

    A) 1990s.   B) 1930s.   C) 1960s.   D) 1950s.

Answer: A
Page Ref: 170
Topic: Factual

6) The 1996 Welfare Reform Act allowed states to contract with for–profit firms to

    A) provide social services.   B) determine benefits.

    C) determine eligibility.   D) all of the above.

Answer: D
Page Ref: 171
Topic: Conceptual

7) The state of Texas experimented with the privatization of social welfare provision and envisioned cutting expenses by 20–40% through all BUT WHICH of the following ways?

    A) incorporating preventative health care benefits

    B) closing offices

    C) eliminating state jobs

    D) privately–run screening of clients

Answer: A
Page Ref: 171
Topic: Applied

8) Which of the following firms did not attempt to run the Texas welfare system?

    A) Dell Computers   B) IBM

    C) Electronic Data Systems   D) Apple Computers

Answer: A
Page Ref: 171
Topic: Factual

9) The authors report that the approximate dollar value of publicly provided goods and services is

    A) $500 billion.   B) $200 billion.   C) $900 billion.   D) $100 million.

Answer: A
Page Ref: 172
Topic: Factual

10) All BUT WHICH of the following comprise foundations ranked as one of the top 20 in assets in the U.S.?

    A) Nancy Dyer Hodge Foundation   B) Lilly Endowment

    C) Ford Foundation   D) Packard Foundation

Answer: A
Page Ref: 181
Topic: Factual

11) Which of the following is not a prominent conservative think tanks?

   A) Brookings Institution   B) American Enterprise Institute
   C) Heritage Foundation   D) Hoover Institution

   Answer: A
   Page Ref: 187
   Topic: Factual

12) Nancye Amidei includes which of the following as responsible business practices?

   A) equitable wages   B) employee rights
   C) environmental responsibility D) all of the above.

   Answer: D
   Page Ref: 189
   Topic: Conceptual

13) There were _____ Human Services Corporations with revenues above $10 million in 2003.

   A) 241   B) 268   C) 50   D) 121

   Answer: A
   Page Ref: 192
   Topic: Factual

14) What percent of the nursing homes in the U. S. are proprietary?

   A) 70   B) 20   C) 50   D) 90

   Answer: A
   Page Ref: 192
   Topic: Factual

15) Which of the following is not a child care proprietary firm?

   A) Kids R Us   B) Kinder Care
   C) Children's Discovery Centers D) Rocking Horse Child Care Centers

   Answer: A
   Page Ref: 195
   Topic: Factual

16) Welfare capitalism was a popular idea among business leaders before World War I.

   Answer: TRUE
   Page Ref: 171
   Topic: Factual

17) Proponents of privatization argue that privatization will lead to cost–effectiveness.

   Answer: TRUE
   Page Ref: 173
   Topic: Factual

18) The standardization of services is an important method for lowering organizational costs.

Answer: TRUE
Page Ref: 174
Topic: Factual

19) Standardization refers to a means of lowering costs of goods and services.

Answer: TRUE
Page Ref: 174
Topic: Conceptual

20) There is clear and convincing evidence that privatization usually leads to greater cost–effectiveness.

Answer: FALSE
Page Ref: 174
Topic: Conceptual

21) Oligolpolization refers to control of markets by a large number of private corporations.

Answer: FALSE
Page Ref: 175
Topic: Factual

22) Public social welfare expenditures grew more rapidly than private SWE from 1980–1992.

Answer: FALSE
Page Ref: 193
Topic: Factual

23) Manor Lane is the largest health care provider of nursing homes in the U.S.

Answer: TRUE
Page Ref: 193
Topic: Factual

24) Kaiser-Permanente is one of the largest for-profit HMO's in the U. S.

Answer: FALSE
Page Ref: 194
Topic: Factual

25) Most analysts expect proprietary correctional facilities to continue to grow.

Answer: FALSE
Page Ref: 197
Topic: Factual

26) What is the role of the business community in U.S. social welfare?

Answer: Historically, business leaders have contributed to U.S. social welfare by: envisaging utopian work environments, providing benefits to employees, fashioning governmental welfare policies, being corporate neighbors and focusing on their duty to care for the community in which they work, subsidizing policy institutes, and shaping current welfare policy.

Page Ref: 169
Topic: Applied

27) To what does the term "privatization" refer?

Answer: This term addresses the idea that private is more efficient than public and should thereby be responsible for the provision of health and human services. More detail is given on page 169 of the text.

Page Ref: 169
Topic: Conceptual

28) What are the three techniques for privatization of services as identified by the President's Commission on Privatization.

Answer: 1. Selling government assets; 2)Contracting with private firms to provide goods and services previously offered by the government; 3)Using vouchers to compensate private providers for services offered.

Page Ref: 169
Topic: Applied

29) What does David Osborne (in "Reinventing Government") suggest for the integration of the public and private sectors? What is your opinion regarding the feasibility of this suggestion?

Answer: That the government should establish the objectives of public policy, assigning the execution to the private sector.

Page Ref: 170
Topic: Applied

30) Discuss at least two advantages of privatization that proponents cite.

Answer: Proponents of privatization argue that it is the most cost-effective and humane way for states to implement welfare reform; deliver technological efficiency by cutting administrative costs and detecting fraud; offering one-stop shopping for benefits and enrollment.

Page Ref: 171
Topic: Applied

31) Discuss at least two of the concerns associated with the privatization of welfare services.

Answer: Opponents argue that if a corporations profits are linked to reducing welfare rolls, the incentive to deny aid will be significant. Additionally, corporations are more apt to reduce personnel costs, encourage the use of technology, as opposed to human work, to save money, the inherent probability of private corporations pulling out of service contracts would leave the federal government with quite a burden; and corporations with a strong presence have a proclivity to shape public policy, which could or could not be in the best interest of beneficiaries.

Page Ref: 171
Topic: Conceptual

32) To what does the concept of preferential selection refer? What are the pros and cons?

Answer: Answers to the latter part of this question will vary, but it is important that students display a grasp of the fact that preferential selection refers to the practice of choosing clients according to criteria of organizational performance, as opposed to client need. Entities that do not practice preferential selection will end up serving a disproportionate number of clients with serious problems and less ability to pay for those problems.

Page Ref: 172
Topic: Applied

33) Explain the concept of corporatization.

Answer: This concept denotes the dependence on the corporate sector to provide welfare.
Page Ref: 173
Topic: Applied

34) Why is the standardization of care within an industry dominated by for-profit firms equated with socialism?

Answer: There are several social consequences of standardized care, one of which is the fact that with this identical treatment of everyone, a one-class social system is created, indicative of a socialist treatment perspective.

Page Ref: 175
Topic: Conceptual

35) Why does the prospect of extensive proprietary involvement in life care trouble some analysts?

Answer: There is a fear that well-funded proprietary interests will "drain off the more financially able segment" of the older population, widening the gap between the "haves" and the "have-nots."

Page Ref: 175
Topic: Applied

36) What are the implications of the oligopolization of human services?

Answer: The control of the market by only a few providers means that competitors will seek to monopolize the market by purchasing their competitors, thereby giving the most powerful and wealthy entities a great advantage at shaping public policy in their areas of interest or service provision.

Page Ref: 175
Topic: Applied

37) How is standardization important to the idea of lowering organizational costs?

Answer: The logic of the market dictates that the goal of production is to process the largest number people at the lowest cost possible, meaning that standardizing care is one of the more important methods for lowering organizational costs.
Page Ref: 175
Topic: Conceptual

38) Why is privatization considered a retreat from a century of hard-won gains in social programs?

Answer: A large-scale shift of public services to private providers would contribute to further isolating the least advantaged, since private firms have strong incentives to skim off the best clients and most profitable services, meaning that the poorest and sickest clients would be relegated to a less attractive, poorer public sector.
Page Ref: 176
Topic: Conceptual

39) Discuss the impact of unions in privatization.

Answer: An in-depth discussion of these impacts can be found on pages 177 & 178 in the text.
Page Ref: 177
Topic: Conceptual

40) How has the privatization of the correctional industry affected that conglomerate cost?

Answer: In depth discussion of privatization in the corrections industry is included on pages 197-198 in the text.
Page Ref: 197
Topic: Conceptual

Chapter 8 The Making of Governmental Policy

1) Which of the following states is the only U.S. member to have a unicameral legislature?

   A) Texas   B) Wyoming   C) California   D) Nebraska

   Answer: D
   Page Ref: 206
   Topic: Factual

2) Of the bills presented in Congress, approximately _____ % are reported out of committee and _____ % become law.

   A) 25; 20   B) 60; 30   C) 10; 5   D) 8; 1

   Answer: C
   Page Ref: 207
   Topic: Factual

3) What piece of legislation requires California lawmakers to have a 2/3 majority in order to raise property taxes and establish that state's fiscal budget?

   A) Proposition 11

   B) California Balanced Budget Amendment

   C) Proposition 13

   D) Article 15

   Answer: C
   Page Ref: 208
   Topic: Factual

4) An elitist orientation asserts that

   A) individuals represent a "power structure" and supports status quo that advantages them, excluding marginal groups.

   B) social policy in a mixed democratic polity is equal opportunity and resultant of trade-offs among different groups, each with the same amount of opportunity.

   C) "bit-by-bit" additions to public social infrastructure produce important and valid questions regarding social policy.

   D) "best practice" evaluations that determine to what extent policy change, effectiveness and outcome studies bring about intended outcomes.

   Answer: A
   Page Ref: 208
   Topic: Conceptual

5) Pluralist orientations assume that

    A) individuals represent a "power structure" and supports status quo that advantages them, excluding marginal groups.

    B) the continued recertification and funding by public decision makers is a sign of an effective and successful program

    C) social policy in a mixed democratic polity is equal opportunity and resultant of trade-offs among different groups, each with the same amount of opportunity.

    D) "best practice" evaluations that determine to what extent policy change, effectiveness and outcome studies bring about intended outcomes.

Answer: C
Page Ref: 209
Topic: Conceptual

6) Incrementalists suggest that

    A) the continued recertification and funding by public decision makers is a sign of an effective and successful program.

    B) individuals represent a "power structure" and supports status quo that advantages them, excluding marginal groups.

    C) "best practice" evaluations that determine to what extent policy change, effectiveness and outcome studies bring about intended outcomes.

    D) "bit-by-bit" additions to public social infrastructure produce important and valid questions regarding social policy.

Answer: D
Page Ref: 209
Topic: Conceptual

7) Rationalists assert that

    A) individuals represent a "power structure" and supports status quo that advantages them, excluding marginal groups.

    B) social policy in a mixed democratic polity is equal opportunity and resultant of trade-offs among different groups, each with the same amount of opportunity.

    C) "bit-by-bit" additions to public social infrastructure produce important and valid questions regarding social policy.

    D) "best practice" evaluations that determine to what extent policy change, effectiveness and outcome studies bring about intended outcomes.

Answer: D
Page Ref: 209
Topic: Conceptual

8) Social activists rely on the premise that

    A) individuals represent a "power structure" and supports status quo that advantages them, excluding marginal groups.

    B) social policy in a mixed democratic polity is equal opportunity and resultant of trade–offs among different groups, each with the same amount of opportunity.

    C) "bit–by–bit" additions to public social infrastructure produce important and valid questions regarding social policy.

    D) the continued recertification and funding by public decision makers is a sign of an effective and successful program.

Answer: D
Page Ref: 209
Topic: Factual

9) Which of the following social philosphers' ideologies is best typified by this statement: "Bureaucracy is a necessary evil for work to be done?"

    A) Plato   B) Karl Marx   C) Alvin Toffler   D) Max Weber

Answer: D
Page Ref: 209
Topic: Applied

10) Which of the following is NOT a central aspect regarding government decision-making?

    A) the degree of change in policy represented by a decision

    B) the rationality of the decision

    C) how the upper and middle class populations benefit

    D) the extent to which the disadvantaged benefit

Answer: C
Page Ref: 209
Topic: Conceptual

11) Which of the following regarding bureaucratic rationality is NOT a true statement?

    A) Civil servants are not able to deploy programs in an equitable and nonpartisan manner.

    B) It is central to governmental policy and hence to the maintenance of the welfare state.

    C) Civil servants can objectively define the social problems they see.

    D) It maintains authority from power vested in the state.

Answer: A
Page Ref: 210
Topic: Conceptual

12) The 1996 welfare reform legislation

    A) exempted 20% of AFDC/TANF caseloads from time limits.

    B) set up special fund accounts for persons 65 years and older, similar to Social Security.

    C) required recipients to work at least 35 hours per week.

    D) all of the above.

Answer: A
Page Ref: 210
Topic: Conceptual

13) Placement of individuals in their social stratification class is usually made on the basis of

    A) income.   B) education.

    C) occupational status.   D) all of the above.

Answer: D
Page Ref: 210
Topic: Factual

14) Which of the following is the most accurate representation of the number of staff members who serve congressional members?

    A) 25,000   B) 5,000

    C) 12,000   D) none of the above

Answer: A
Page Ref: 210
Topic: Factual

15) At the federal level, the primary committee dealing with social welfare in 2000 was the

    A) Senate Finance Committee.   B) House Ways and Means Committee.

    C) House Appropriations Committee.   D) all of the above.

Answer: D
Page Ref: 211
Topic: Factual

16) As in the upper levels of the judiciary, members in municipal courts also hold their posts for life.

Answer: FALSE
Page Ref: 206
Topic: Conceptual

17) The process of creating legislation is a difficult one and usually ends unsuccessfully.

Answer: TRUE
Page Ref: 206
Topic: Factual

18) Working class and under class citizens have little representation in the formulation stage of the legislative process.

Answer: TRUE
Page Ref: 207
Topic: Factual

19) In the federal government, all proposals related to taxation must originate in the U.S. Senate.

Answer: FALSE
Page Ref: 207
Topic: Factual

20) The liberal evolutionary perspective emphasizes the differences between organized groups that compete for social resources — social policy and resultant programs are the products of intense rivalry among various classes and groups.

Answer: FALSE
Page Ref: 209
Topic: Factual

21) Most social policy changes consist of relatively minor technical adjustments in program administration and budgeting.

Answer: TRUE
Page Ref: 210
Topic: Factual

22) Market rationality refers to the ordering of social affairs by governmental agencies.

Answer: FALSE
Page Ref: 210
Topic: Factual

23) Only about 10% of Americans get their health and welfare needs met through employer-provided benefits.

Answer: FALSE
Page Ref: 210
Topic: Factual

24) The 1996 welfare reform legislation ended the 60-year entitlement to income for poor families on the basis of evaluations of state welfare demonstrations allegedly showing that states could provide public assistance better if the federal government were not involved.

Answer: TRUE
Page Ref: 210
Topic: Conceptual

25) In today's society, policy formulation begins with the legislative phase.

Answer: FALSE
Page Ref: 211
Topic: Conceptual

26) Discuss how an idea becomes legislation. In your opinion what is the most important phase of the process?

Answer: The first part of the question is essentially a "sum up" of the entire chapter. Ensure that students have a firm grasp and are able to articulate that the process is long and arduous and often unsuccessful. Answers will vary to part 2.
Page Ref: 206
Topic: Applied

27) Remember one social philosopher named in the book and discuss his/her ideology regarding the policy process and the existence of power.

Answer: From Plato to Machiavelli, to Hobbes, Locke, and Weber, students will have a variety of different answers. For reference, see pages 8–8 through 8–9.
Page Ref: 208
Topic: Conceptual

28) Identify and discuss the five different schools of thought regarding social organization and policy.

Answer: Students should be able to name elitist, pluralist, incrementalist, rationalist, and social activist as the five schools of thought. For elaboration on what each of these tenets assert, see pages 8–8 and 8–9.
Page Ref: 209
Topic: Factual

29) List and give a brief description of the two orientations regarding the nature of social policy and how it is interpreted.

Answer: Students will be able to provide you with "liberal" and "conservative," as obvious answers. See pages 8–9 and 8–10 for further explanation.
Page Ref: 209
Topic: Factual

30) Discuss the two social planning methods in regard to their ability to anticipate future problems and deal with current problems.

Answer: Technomethodological planning emphasizes databases, sophisticated social research methods and work best with programs that can be quantified and routinized. Sociopolitical planning approaches are interactive, interpersonal and community focused efforts.
Page Ref: 210
Topic: Conceptual

31) Discuss the four stages of the policy process.

Answer: Students should expound on the following: Formulation, legislation, implementation, and evaluation.

Page Ref: 211
Topic: Applied

32) Explain why poor and minority populations are currently not well represented by PACs and lobbyists.

Answer: Students will have a variety of opinions on this matter, but all answers should include the fact that these groups do not have the financial support necessary to retain lobbyists, relying primarily on volunteers.

Page Ref: 218
Topic: Conceptual

33) When a policy is enacted, does this ensure implementation? Why or why not?

Answer: No. Ensure that students are able to talk about continuing barriers to policy implementation, including the failure to provide for adequate authority, personnel, or funding to accomplish its stated purpose.

Page Ref: 220
Topic: Applied

34) What federal agencies exist primarily to evaluate programs? Describe how these entities operate.

Answer: Students should be able to list: General Accounting Office (GAO), Office of Management and Budget (OMB), Congressional Budget Office (CBO), and the Congressional Research Service (CRS).

Page Ref: 220
Topic: Conceptual

35) In program evaluation, it is important that researchers maintain and proceed with as little bias as possible. What are some problems with this statement that the text addresses?

Answer: The text addresses the fact that many of these evaluators are former government officials, capitalizing on their connections, impartial evaluators, nepotism, etc.

Page Ref: 220
Topic: Conceptual

36) Why is the measure of unemployment often viewed as inaccurate?

Answer: Answers will vary, but each student should include the fact that underemployed and discouraged workers, as well as part-time workers are not included in the cited statistics, making the numbers much lower than they actually are.

Page Ref: 221
Topic: Conceptual

37) Discuss the role of social workers in social reform movements during and since the Progressive era.

Answer: Students should point to the fact that social workers are omnipresent and often times catalyst for social change. Any social workers mentioned on page 224 would be appropriate.

Page Ref: 223
Topic: Applied

38) Discuss two of the attributes labeled "the nature of U.S. culture" in the text that make formulating social work policy a "complicated and arduous task."

Answer: Students should be able to expound upon two of the following: competing interests, multiple systems of government that compete for funds and write policy, large constituencies served by these groups, economic and technologic developments that lead to specialization.

Page Ref: 225
Topic: Applied

39) Discuss what the authors' mean when they write "Who controls the means of analysis?" regarding social work policy.

Answer: If social workers are to shape social policy as effectively as they have in the past, they will have to learn to control the means of analysis. This means conducting research on social problems, surveying public opinion, analyzing existing social policies and winning elected office.

Page Ref: 226
Topic: Conceptual

40) Discuss the role of advocacy organizations and policy institutes in shaping public policy. Name three of these entities mentioned in the text.

Answer: Students' selection of entities will vary, but each of these plays a very important role in the shaping of social policy as they advocate, debate and raise money for important causes such as children's welfare, budget priorities, and minority groups, among others.

Page Ref: 226
Topic: Conceptual

Chapter 9 Tax Policy and Income Distribution

1) An example of a targeted tax expenditure is
   A) refundable tax credits.   B) direct social services.
   C) in-kind benefits.   D) works programs.

   Answer: A
   Page Ref: 233
   Topic: Factual

2) What piece of legislation effectively created what we know now as the "welfare state?"
   A) Personal Responsibility and Work Opportunity Reconciliation Act
   B) Equal Pay Act of 1963
   C) Social Security Act of 1935
   D) Fair Employment Practices Committee of 1935

   Answer: C
   Page Ref: 233
   Topic: Conceptual

3) What does the phrase, "showdown at Gucci gulch" refer to?
   A) President Reagan's legislative assistants
   B) Lobbyists on Washington's K Street
   C) Hillary Clinton in the early debates of universal health care coverage
   D) Lobbyists in support of Bush's PRWORA

   Answer: B
   Page Ref: 234
   Topic: Factual

4) What Constitutional Amendment initiated the federal income tax?
   A) 19th   B) 12th   C) 14th   D) 16th

   Answer: D
   Page Ref: 234
   Topic: Factual

5) The Federal Income Tax is
   A) progressive.   B) regressive.
   C) inconsequential.   D) retroactive.

   Answer: A
   Page Ref: 234
   Topic: Factual

6) The EITC is

    A) available to all taxpayers.

    B) an educational credit available to students.

    C) a refundable tax credit.

    D) all of the above.

Answer: C
Page Ref: 234
Topic: Factual

7) The Earned Income Tax Credit (EITC) is

    A) increasing in bi–partisan support.

    B) a refundable tax credit.

    C) providing much–needed child care tax refunds for the middle class.

    D) being phased out as a result of the Bush Administration's 2004 tax plan.

Answer: B
Page Ref: 234
Topic: Factual

8) The social security income tax is

    A) progressive.

    B) regressive.

    C) inconsequential.

    D) responsible for funding social welfare programs such as TANF and CHIPs.

Answer: B
Page Ref: 234
Topic: Factual

9) What is the primary element of federal tax policy?

    A) Income tax   B) Social Security   C) EITC   D) all of the above

Answer: D
Page Ref: 234
Topic: Factual

10) In 2004, the fourth income quintile paid only _____ % of the individual income tax revenue in the United States in comparison to the top quintile's _____ %.

    A) 5; 85

    B) 15; 85

    C) 20; 80

    D) Due to the Bush Administration's 2004 tax cuts, the top and fourth quintiles paid the same amount, which was increasingly lower than in the Clinton terms.

Answer: B
Page Ref: 235
Topic: Factual

11) In 2004, the highest income quintile claimed almost _____ % of income accrued in the United States.

    A) 60   B) 70   C) 40   D) 35

Answer: A
Page Ref: 235
Topic: Factual

12) In 2004, the lowest income quintile paid less than 5% of the nation's tax revenue in what category?

    A) Payroll tax   B) Individual Income tax

    C) Estate tax   D) All of the above

Answer: D
Page Ref: 235
Topic: Factual

13) In what year did the generation known as the "Baby Boomers" begin collecting on social security benefits?

    A) 1994   B) 2000   C) 2008   D) 2050

Answer: C
Page Ref: 236
Topic: Factual

14) The estimated number of poor Americans (in millions) if there were no safety net programs:

    A) 34   B) 54   C) 74   D) 100

Answer: B
Page Ref: 241
Topic: Factual

15) What is the type of safety net program that removes the greatest number of Americans from poverty?

    A) in-kind benefits   B) means-tested cash

    C) social insurance   D) works programs

Answer: C
Page Ref: 241
Topic: Factual

16) Tax policy is truly of inconsequential interest to advocates of social justice.

Answer: FALSE
Page Ref: 233
Topic: Conceptual

17) The Reagan presidency showed a marked change in tax policy, increasing economic inequality.

Answer: TRUE
Page Ref: 233
Topic: Factual

18) Moxt taxpayers now pay more in income tax than they do for Social Security withholding.

Answer: FALSE
Page Ref: 234
Topic: Factual

19) Economic policy has little influence on social programming.

Answer: FALSE
Page Ref: 234
Topic: Conceptual

20) By 1983, the annual deficit was almost 7% of gross national product.

Answer: TRUE
Page Ref: 236
Topic: Factual

21) As a primary response to the national debt, legislators in the early 1990s capped spending on international priorities.

Answer: FALSE
Page Ref: 236
Topic: Factual

22) The Clinton social investment plan was projected to produce a budget surplus of only $25 million over 1 year.

Answer: FALSE
Page Ref: 236
Topic: Factual

23) Republican control of the Congress in the year 2000 put tax policy as one of its primary concerns.

Answer: TRUE
Page Ref: 236
Topic: Factual

24) The Social Security program is not capable of sustaining the population known as "Baby Boomers" throughout their lifetime.

Answer: TRUE
Page Ref: 236
Topic: Factual

25) The largest tax credits available for low income tax payers in 2003 was approximately 10 times the expenditure for middle class tax payers.

Answer: FALSE
Page Ref: 237
Topic: Factual

26) What is meant by Harry Hopkins' statement: "Tax, tax, spend, spend, elect, elect!"

Answer: Students' answers should follow along the lines of the fact that this is a methodology espoused by liberals to provide social services to all citizens. Wealthy are taxed at a higher rate, revenues are diverted to social programs, and social program beneficiaries show their appreciation by voting Democrat.
Page Ref: 233
Topic: Conceptual

27) Discuss the three tax policies central to U.S. social policy.

Answer: Students should expound on the following three answers: income and withholding taxes, and the earned income tax credit.
Page Ref: 234
Topic: Conceptual

28) Describe Arthur Laffer's "optimal economic policy."

Answer: Laffer subscribed to the belief that minimal taxation would keep capital formation and expansion from being halted. This was a very "Reaganomics" ideology.
Page Ref: 234
Topic: Conceptual

29) Does tax policy currently benefit special interest groups? Why or why not?

Answer: Special interest groups, namely corporations, are often able to "bend" the tax code to their benefit, including diverting funds, avoiding heavy taxation with charitable donations, etc. Student answers will vary, but it is essential that they display knowledge of the fact that the powerful and wealthy benefit often under current U.S. tax code.
Page Ref: 237
Topic: Conceptual

30) How does tax law affect the revenues of nonprofit organizations.

Answer: By allowing taxpayers to deduct charitable contributions from taxable income, lower tax rates give more discretionary income that could, in theory, be applied toward charitable donations, etc.
Page Ref: 237
Topic: Applied

31) What factors account for the low tax rate in the U.S. in comparison to other OECD (Organization for Economic Cooperation and Development) nations?

Answer: An in-depth discussion of these variables can be found on pages 238 through 240.
Page Ref: 238
Topic: Applied

32) Why are state income taxes important?

Answer: States hold major responsiblity for social welfare programs, such as mental health, child welfare, and corrections. State tax policy also establishes an income floor for taxation or exempts low-income families from tax liability altogether.
Page Ref: 240
Topic: Conceptual

33) According to the text, what makes the "biggest dent in poverty" and why?

Answer: The text purports, and many experts agree, that social insurance (ie compulsory contributions to Social Security and Medicare) contributes more than twice that of public assistance cash and in-kind benefits.
Page Ref: 240
Topic: Factual

34) Discuss the meaning of the tables included on page 242 & 243 for wealthy individuals? poor individuals?

Answer: Obviously, the use of this question will require the that you include the table in your exam. This can be a wonderful exercise in data interpretation and answers will vary, but should speak to the fact that poorer individuals receive more benefits in the areas of housing, health care and income security, and their upper income counterparts benefit primarily in economic affairs and education.
Page Ref: 242
Topic: Conceptual

35) Discuss at least three tax credits available to the poor and how these affect direct income transfers.

Answer: The list of tax credits includes the EITC, child care, welfare-to-work, elder care, disabled care, adoption expenses. As a number of tax credits have increased, tax credits have emerged as a contender to replace, at least partially, direct income transfers to aid the poor.
Page Ref: 244
Topic: Factual

36) Discuss at least three policy issues raised by the replacement of welfare transfers with tax credits.

Answer: See page 244 for a complete listing and discussion of these issues.
Page Ref: 244
Topic: Applied

37) In GUNS, GERMS, & STEEL, Jared Diamond states: "These noble and selfish functions are inextricably linked, although some governments emphasize much more of one function than of the other. The difference between a kleptomaniac and a wise statesman, between a robber baron and a public benefactor is merely one of degree: a matter of just how large a percentage of the the tribute extracted from producers is retained by the elite,and how much the commoners like the public uses to which the redistributed tribute is put." Agree of disagree with this statement and explain why you took this stance.

Answer: Student answers will vary as opinions on this statement will. Make sure, however, that students exemplify a sound understanding of what this quotation means, that all societies try to balance the provision of essential services with measures aimed at thwarting the "kleptomaniac inclinations" of those in power.

Page Ref: 246
Topic: Conceptual

38) How does classic liberalism critique government taxation. Do you agree or disagree with this theory? Why or why not.

Answer: Answers to the latter question will vary, but students should exhibit a degree of understanding regarding the fact that classic liberalism emphasizes the freedom of individuals to act in their own best interests.

Page Ref: 246
Topic: Applied

39) Is poverty "genetic?" Using ideology presented in Chapter 9, as well as your own opinions, formulate your answer.

Answer: Answers will vary, but students should be able to demonstrate their knowledge regarding the fact that poverty is, often times, cyclical.

Page Ref: 247
Topic: Conceptual

40) What is "bootstrap capitalism?"

Answer: The theory that capitalist nations tend to have citing that instead of welfare, the impoverished or oppressed populations simply need to "pull themselves up by the bootstraps." This sentiment, however, does not address the fact that many times, the individual does not even own boots.

Page Ref: 249
Topic: Conceptual

Chapter 10 Social Insurance Programs

1) Social insurance programs cost $ _____ in 2002, public assistance programs cost $ _____.
   A) 978 million; 1 billion   B) 250 billion; 906 billion
   C) 773 billion; 308 billion   D) 125 billion; 25 billion

   Answer: C
   Page Ref: 252
   Topic: Factual

2) It is estimated that the Federal Government will spend $ _____ on Medicare in 2010.
   A) 287 billion   B) 482 million   C) 366 billion   D) 421 billion

   Answer: D
   Page Ref: 252
   Topic: Factual

3) In 2001, Social Security accounted for what percent of the GDP?
   A) less than 5%   B) over 30%   C) 25%   D) 14%

   Answer: A
   Page Ref: 253
   Topic: Factual

4) The average monthly OASDI benefit in 2003 was:
   A) $598.   B) $1,150.   C) $798.   D) $998.

   Answer: B
   Page Ref: 253
   Topic: Factual

5) In 2001, social insurance programs accounted for _____ % of the total federal budget.
   A) 6   B) 22   C) 11   D) 35

   Answer: D
   Page Ref: 253
   Topic: Factual

6) The approximate poverty rate for the elderly is:
   A) 15%.   B) 10%.   C) 30%.   D) 25%.

   Answer: B
   Page Ref: 255
   Topic: Factual

7) In what year did the U.S. government begin its Federal Employment Retirement program?

   A) 1961   B) 1935   C) 1920   D) 1915

   Answer: C
   Page Ref: 253
   Topic: Factual

8) In 2001, unemployment compensation accounted for what percentage of the GDP?

   A) 20   B) 14   C) 5   D) .3

   Answer: D
   Page Ref: 253
   Topic: Factual

9) The 1935 Social Security Act assisted all BUT WHICH of the following populations?

   A) disabled   B) dependent children

   C) blind   D) elderly

   Answer: A
   Page Ref: 253
   Topic: Conceptual

10) In what year was Medicare incorporated into law?

   A) 1965   B) 1935   C) 1929   D) 1949

   Answer: A
   Page Ref: 254
   Topic: Factual

11) Whatpercentof U.S. households depended on a monthly Social Security check in 1996?

   A) 5   B) 25   C) 35   D) 10

   Answer: B
   Page Ref: 254
   Topic: Factual

12) In 2002, the Social Security trust funds earned $ _____ in interest.

   A) 80 billion   B) 100 million   C) 13 billion   D) 72 million

   Answer: A
   Page Ref: 255
   Topic: Factual

13) Part–time workers are _____% less likely than full time workers to collect unemployment insurance.

   A) 76   B) 59   C) 42   D) 88

   Answer: B
   Page Ref: 257
   Topic: Factual

14) The approximate poverty rate for the elderly in 1996 if there were no Social Security income:

    A) 52%.   B) 42%.   C) 22%.   D) 32%.

Answer: A
Page Ref: 260
Topic: Factual

15) Social Security benefits will begin to exceed tax collections in

    A) 2015   B) 2007   C) 2009   D) 2050

Answer: A
Page Ref: 262
Topic: Factual

16) Social insurance is financed through payroll and other taxes.

Answer: TRUE
Page Ref: 252
Topic: Factual

17) The major goal of social insurance is to help maintain income by replacing a portion of lost earnings.

Answer: TRUE
Page Ref: 252
Topic: Factual

18) Social security has taken on some of the characteristics of an income redistribution and public assistance program.

Answer: TRUE
Page Ref: 252
Topic: Factual

19) Like Social Security, public assistance programs are subject to means tests.

Answer: FALSE
Page Ref: 252
Topic: Conceptual

20) Most social insurance programs tend to be stigmatized as much as social welfare policies.

Answer: FALSE
Page Ref: 252
Topic: Conceptual

21) The first old-age insurance program was introduced in Germany in 1889.

Answer: TRUE
Page Ref: 253
Topic: Factual

22) Supplemental Security Income (SSI), like Social Security is a "pay as you go" program.

Answer: FALSE
Page Ref: 254
Topic: Conceptual

23) Old Age and Survivors Insurance and Disability insurance (OASDI) covers approximately 9 out of 10 workers.

Answer: TRUE
Page Ref: 255
Topic: Factual

24) In 2002, the poverty rate for the elderly was slightly higher than for that of the general population.

Answer: FALSE
Page Ref: 255
Topic: Factual

25) The current guidelines of the UI program require employers and employees to contribute to a trust fund, activated only when an employee loses his/her job.

Answer: FALSE
Page Ref: 256
Topic: Factual

26) For what does the current Social Security Act provide?

Answer: As amended, the Social Security Act provides for: OASDI, UI programs under joint federal and state programs, federal assistance to aged, blind and disabled persons, TANF, Medicare, and Medicaid.
Page Ref: 253
Topic: Factual

27) Discuss the trust funds into which Social Security and Medicare are divided. Include the names and mechanisms of governance.

Answer: Funds and governance are discussed in detail on page 254 of the text.
Page Ref: 254
Topic: Conceptual

28) Give at least two reasons that Social Security is considered a "stellar example of a program that has worked."

Answer: In 2002, SS served more than 50 million people and upwards of 4 million people were awarded benefits; 65% of the aged population received at least half of their income; SS kept 39% of aged persons out of poverty; Women accounted for 57% of adult SS beneficiaries.
Page Ref: 255
Topic: Applied

29) What do political conservatives dislike about Social Security?

Answer: They dislike the fact that it socializes a portion of the national income.
Page Ref: 256
Topic: Conceptual

30) Describe how the unemployment benefits system operates. Who is eligible and for how long?

Answer: In depth descriptions of UI benefits are described on page 257 in the text.
Page Ref: 257
Topic: Factual

31) Discuss five of the problems associated with unemployment insurance.

Answer: Nine problems are addressed in regard to issues with our current UI program. An in-depth discussion can be found on page 257 in the text.
Page Ref: 257
Topic: Conceptual

32) What are the special problems women face with unemployment?

Answer: Women are faced with special issues in the workplace, as well as on UI. Women are more than likely than their male counterparts to be part time workers, thus earning less wages and potentially being ineligible for the minimum earnings to qualify. Only 39% of unemployed women receive UI, as opposed to 41% of men.
Page Ref: 258
Topic: Applied

33) What is one suggested reform for UI?

Answer: An individual unemployment account is one option which transfers the burden of UI from the employer to the employee, allowing them to choose the option of setting a portion of their earnings aside & made available to the worker anytime he or she was out of a job.
Page Ref: 258
Topic: Applied

34) Is worker's compensation considered problematic in any way? Support and depend your answer.

Answer: Yes. 1) Benefit levels are established on the basis of state formulas and are usually calculated at a percentage of weekly earnings and these levels vary greatly from state to state. 2) The cost to employers to provide WC is rising rapidly. 3)There is also great variablity in the way that state's handle and process WC claims 4)There are often long delays between when an injury occurs and when compensation is given. 5) Finally, WC may not provide adequate coverage for the disabled.
Page Ref: 259
Topic: Applied

35) What are the three major social insurance programs in the U.S.?

Answer: They are: 1) OASDI; 2) UI; & 3) Workers' Compensation
Page Ref: 259
Topic: Factual

36) How is Social Security exacerbating intergenerational tensions?

Answer: Many in younger generations feel that they are paying into a system they will never receive anything out of, causing feelings of animosity toward those who are fully utilizing the system now. As poignantly stated by Ted Dimig in the Houston Chronicle, It "leaves us with a huge resentment over the idea that our elders might saddle us with the debt for their retirement, while shortchanging us on our own retirement."
Page Ref: 260
Topic: Applied

37) What are the long term prospects for Social Security?

Answer: Answers will vary, including that Social Security is projected to sustain itself, and some answers arguing that the Baby Boomer retirement period will exhaust an already-overburdened system. Answers should all, however, include some of the prospects discussed in detail on pages 262 & 263.
Page Ref: 262
Topic: Conceptual

38) Give a basic overview of Bush's plan to remedy the Social Security problem.

Answer: The Bush plan restructures the SS program to allow workers under 55 divert a portion of their SS payroll taxes into private investment accounts in exchange for lower guaranteed future benefits. Workers would not be able to leave the personal account system once they enter into it. T he Bush plan operates under the assumption that because Social Security taxes belong to the worker, the worker should be able to do with them as he/she sees fit.
Page Ref: 265
Topic: Conceptual

39) What are the mechanics of the Partial Privatization Plan and what are the options included within the plan?

Answer: The PPP is a publicly administered plan, modeled on the Thrift Savings Plan and allows employees to choose from five mutual funds. Funds cannot be withdrawn prior to retirement and cost considerations for this plan are estimated to be as high as $2 trillion over 10 years.
Page Ref: 265
Topic: Applied

40) What are perceived risks to Bush's plan?

Answer: As with any investment venture, there is a chance that investments will "go south" and the worker or investor will be left with nothing. Should an acute economic downturn occur and workers' accounts be wiped out, the Federal Government would, more than likely, have to shoulder the burden of caring for some of these workers in their old age, should they become impoverished. Taxes and bonds, as used currently, are virtually risk free.

Page Ref: 266
Topic: Conceptual

Chapter 11 Public Assistance Programs

1) A majority of federal dollars are spent on

    A) income security programs.   B) debt interest.

    C) military defense.   D) health care.

Answer: C
Page Ref: 270
Topic: Factual

2) The average size of TANF families in 1999 (parent and children):

    A) 2   B) 7   C) 5   D) 3

Answer: D
Page Ref: 271
Topic: Factual

3) The TANF rolls between 1996 and 2001

    A) increased dramatically.   B) stayed the same.

    C) increased slightly.   D) decreased.

Answer: D
Page Ref: 271
Topic: Factual

4) The percent of those eligible who actually receive TANF benefits:

    A) 69   B) 52   C) 33   D) 42

Answer: B
Page Ref: 271
Topic: Factual

5) The percent of TANF recipients who are able-bodied adult males:

    A) 1   B) 5   C) 40   D) 15

Answer: A
Page Ref: 271
Topic: Factual

6) In 2003, the average 3-person TANF family received a monthly benefit of $_____.

    A) 700   B) 1,000   C) 200   D) 355

Answer: A
Page Ref: 273
Topic: Factual

7) In 2002, the average monthly SSI benefit was

    A) $770.   B) $989.   C) $227.   D) $407.

Answer: D
Page Ref: 282
Topic: Factual

8) The percent of SSI recipients who were disabled:

    A) 60   B) 20   C) 80   D) 40

Answer: C
Page Ref: 282
Topic: Factual

9) The amount of resources which will disqualify a person from receiving SSI benefits:

    A) $5,001   B) $4,001   C) $3,001   D) $2,001

Answer: D
Page Ref: 282
Topic: Factual

10) The number of SSI recipients in 2002, in millions:

    A) 16.5   B) 4.1   C) 11.9   D) 6.8

Answer: D
Page Ref: 282
Topic: Factual

11) The number of states that have General Assistance Programs:

    A) 35   B) 45   C) 51   D) 25

Answer: A
Page Ref: 283
Topic: Factual

12) The percent of births to teens that occur outside of marriage:

    A) 68   B) 20   C) 31   D) 58

Answer: C
Page Ref: 287
Topic: Factual

13) What percentage of recipients who leave welfare return at some point?

    A) 25   B) 75

    C) 50   D) none of the above

Answer: B
Page Ref: 272
Topic: Factual

14) What is thought to be the best predictor of welfare dependency?

    A) age at entry to welfare   B) previous work experience

    C) number of children   D) all of the above

Answer: D
Page Ref: 272
Topic: Conceptual

15) The percentage of work participation among TANF recipients in 2001 was:

    A) 15   B) 45   C) 30   D) 100

Answer: B
Page Ref: 277
Topic: Factual

16) Teenage birth rates have declined steadily since 1991.

Answer: TRUE
Page Ref: 287
Topic: Factual

17) Teenage birth rates in the U. S. are higher than those in most developed countries.

Answer: TRUE
Page Ref: 287
Topic: Factual

18) Teens who give birth are more likely to come from poor families.

Answer: TRUE
Page Ref: 287
Topic: Factual

19) White and Black adolescents experienced declines in pregnancy in the 1990s.

Answer: TRUE
Page Ref: 288
Topic: Factual

20) Public assistance in the U.S. is a relatively coordinated system.

Answer: FALSE
Page Ref: 270
Topic: Applied

21) States have little freedom to fashion their own safety nets for poverty, much of the requirements are mandated by federal regulation.

Answer: FALSE
Page Ref: 271
Topic: Factual

22) Overall, the percentage of the poor receiving welfare has declined since the early 1970s.

Answer: TRUE
Page Ref: 271
Topic: Factual

23) Statistics show that less than 30% of women from heavily-dependent welfare homes were heavily-dependent on welfare themselves.

Answer: TRUE
Page Ref: 272
Topic: Factual

24) The largest percentage of welfare recipients are black.

Answer: TRUE
Page Ref: 273
Topic: Factual

25) The single largest predictor of beginning welfare is a divorce or separation.

Answer: TRUE
Page Ref: 273
Topic: Factual

26) Name and describe the major public assistance programs in U.S. social welfare policy.

Answer: TANF, SSI and General Assistance are three of the major public assistance programs in the U.S. Students should be able to exhibit firm understanding of the roles and requirements of each.
Page Ref: 270
Topic: Applied

27) Discuss three of the hostile assumptions that underlie the discussion surrounding public assistance.

Answer: The text suggests 5 assumptions that underlie public assistance discussions, including: 1)generous benefits create a disincentive to work; 2)welfare recipients need prodding to work b/c they lack internal motivation; 3)work is the best antipoverty measure; 4)We must stigmatize public assistance programs, lest people turn to them too quickly; 5)Women receiving public assistance should work; impoverished children should not have the luxury of having a stay-at-home mother.
Page Ref: 270
Topic: Applied

28) Using information from class and the text, dispel the following myth regarding public assistance: "It is easy to get on public assistance & too many undeserving people are receiving benefits."

Answer: Student answers will vary, however, the general theme should address the fact that the process of applying for and receiving welfare is arduous and difficult. IN addition, only about 25% of those who apply receive benefits like food stamps and families are often dropped at the first sign of non-compliance.

Page Ref: 273
Topic: Applied

29) Do TANF benefits influence decisions relating to family composition by encouraging women to head their own households? Why or why not?

Answer: Under TANF guidelines, women under 18 are not eligible for benefits unless they are living at home or a supervised facility. There is conflicting evidence and studies regarding whether or not this is a legitimate phenomena exist. See page 274 for further information.

Page Ref: 274
Topic: Conceptual

30) Discuss the evolution of the AFDC program, mentioning key dates in its development.

Answer: AFDC was first initiated in 1935 in the Social Security Act of that same year. SInce then it has developed into TANF and more information regarding the people and dates associated with the program, see pages 274–276.

Page Ref: 275
Topic: Factual

31) Discuss the major components of the Family Support Act.

Answer: The FSA attempted to change AFDC from an income support to a mandatory work and training program. The FSA established the JOBS program, requiring recipient women with children under 3 to participate in a job training program. As an incentive to enroll, participants received 12 months of child care assistance and Medicaid benefits. Support and thus efficacy of the FSA faded, with funds being ill spent and cases outnumbering available workers.

Page Ref: 275
Topic: Applied

32) What was the major distinction between AFDC and TANF as mandated by the PRWORA. What were the implications.

Answer: See page 276 for an in-depth comparison and contrast between these two programs.
Page Ref: 276
Topic: Conceptual

33) What are the four specific work requirements as delineated in the TANF block grant.

Answer: 1) Unless the state opts out, it must require nonexempt unemployed parents or caregivers to participate in community service after receiving assistance for two months; 2)States must outline how they will require a parent or caregiver receiving benefits to engage in work not later than 24 months after they receive assistance. 3) A state must meet a work participation rate for all families that began at 25 in 1997 and increasing to 50 percent beyond 2002. 4) States must meet different participation rates for two-parent families.

Page Ref: 277
Topic: Factual

34) Discuss the merits of the conservative push toward labor policy.

Answer: Removing the federal responsibility for providing long-term cash assistance to the poor shifted the problem of poor support away from social welfare and into labor policy. This push has merit, including the fact that U.S. public assistance policy has been reduced to a short-term, transitional step in the march toward full labor market participation of the poor. Reasons for this push are discussed on page 286.

Page Ref: 286
Topic: Conceptual

35) To what group of people does the term "hard to employ" refer?

Answer: This group of people has significant barriers to work and difficulty in finding and sustaining work. Some of the barriers may included language, substance abuse, disability, mental health, chronic health problems, etc.

Page Ref: 287
Topic: Conceptual

36) Name at least two economic consequences for women choosing to have children out of wedlock.

Answer: This pervasive national problem is discussed in greater detail on pages 288 and 289 in the text.

Page Ref: 288
Topic: Factual

37) Why is the anti teen pregnancy movement so politicized? What are arguments on both sides.

Answer: One side argues for comprehensive sex education, promoting abstinence, but including information about contraception. There are other programs that promote abstinence-only education. These two sides argue over what is the legal and moral obligation of the government, as well as which programs are more effective in decreasing teenage pregnancy.

Page Ref: 289
Topic: Conceptual

38) What are the four groups who make up the "underclass?"

Answer: The four groups are the: 1) passive poor, usually dependent on welfare; 2)hostile street predators, often dropouts and addicts; 3)hustlers or opportunists who do not commit violent crimes and 4) the traumatized who are the victims of deinstitutionalization.
Page Ref: 289
Topic: Factual

39) How is TANF considered a form of welfare behaviorism?

Answer: It is an attempt to reprogram the behaviors of the poor.
Page Ref: 289
Topic: Conceptual

40) How does PRWORA reflect an attitude of personal and parental responsibility?

Answer: See reasons (5) listed on page 290 for a further discussion.
Page Ref: 290
Topic: Conceptual

Chapter 12   The American Health Care System

1) Approximately how many million Americans lack health insurance coverage?

   A) 60   B) 10   C) 22   D) 45

   Answer: D
   Page Ref: 302
   Topic: Factual

2) Approximately what percentage of Americans do have health insurance coverage?

   A) 55   B) 85   C) 45   D) 15

   Answer: B
   Page Ref: 302
   Topic: Factual

3) Most health care costs in the U. S. are paid by

   A) private insurers.   B) government supplements.

   C) public insurers.   D) out-of-pocket payment.

   Answer: A
   Page Ref: 303
   Topic: Factual

4) The annual cost of family health insurance premiums in 2004 was

   A) $2,400.   B) $4,800.   C) $9,300.   D) $6,300.

   Answer: C
   Page Ref: 303
   Topic: Factual

5) Medicaid was enacted in

   A) 1965.   B) 1980.   C) 1976.   D) 1935.

   Answer: A
   Page Ref: 304
   Topic: Factual

6) Among social insurance programs, Medicare is the

   A) 3rd largest.   B) largest.   C) smallest.   D) 2nd largest.

   Answer: D
   Page Ref: 304
   Topic: Factual

7) Medicare served approximately how many million people in 2003?

    A) 61   B) 41   C) 25   D) 100

Answer: B
Page Ref: 304
Topic: Factual

8) Since 1991 Medicare expenditures have grown from $100 billion to approximately $_____ in 2002.

    A) 101 billion   B) 500 billion   C) 266 billion   D) 150 billion

Answer: C
Page Ref: 304
Topic: Factual

9) Medicare is primarily funded by

    A) state government.   B) federal government.

    C) both.   D) employees and employers.

Answer: B
Page Ref: 304
Topic: Factual

10) In 2002, the CHIP program covers 5.3 million children; expenditures for this program were approximately _____.

    A) 100 billion   B) 100 million   C) 82.3 billion   D) 5.3 billion

Answer: D
Page Ref: 312
Topic: Factual

11) In 2004, national health expenditures in the U.S. were approximately

    A) $1.2 trillion.   B) $100 billion.   C) $500 billion.   D) $1.8 trillion.

Answer: D
Page Ref: 314
Topic: Factual

12) The major source of revenue for U. S. health costs is

    A) Medicare.   B) private insurance.

    C) out-of-pocket.   D) Medicaid.

Answer: B
Page Ref: 315
Topic: Factual

13) Approximate median per-capita health expenditures (2000) by OECD countries were

    A) $4,000.   B) $2,000.   C) $10,000.   D) $1,000.

Answer: B
Page Ref: 315
Topic: Factual

14) Approximate median per-capita health expenditures (2000) by the U. S. were

    A) $4,000.   B) $2,000.   C) $1,000.   D) $1,700.

Answer: A
Page Ref: 315
Topic: Factual

15) Out-of-pocket per capita health care spending in the U.S. in 2000 was approximately

    A) $700.   B) $200.   C) $900.   D) $5,000.

Answer: A
Page Ref: 315
Topic: Factual

16) The population group least likely to have health insurance are those aged 18-24.

Answer: TRUE
Page Ref: 302
Topic: Factual

17) In 2001, the cost of medical care for the uninsured totaled about $100 billion.

Answer: TRUE
Page Ref: 303
Topic: Factual

18) The dominant form of health care coverage in the U. S. is private insurance.

Answer: TRUE
Page Ref: 303
Topic: Factual

19) Medicare and Medicaid are Social Security Act programs.

Answer: TRUE
Page Ref: 304
Topic: Factual

20) Medicare is a public assistance program.

Answer: FALSE
Page Ref: 304
Topic: Factual

21) Medicaid is a social insurance program.

Answer: FALSE
Page Ref: 304
Topic: Factual

22) Under the Medicare legislation, drugs can only be reimported from Mexico.

Answer: FALSE
Page Ref: 305
Topic: Factual

23) Two–thirds of doctor visits in the U.S. result in a drug being prescribed.

Answer: TRUE
Page Ref: 318
Topic: Factual

24) Canada's prospective global budgeting system for hospitals is said to have caused severe health care rationing.

Answer: TRUE
Page Ref: 328
Topic: Conceptual

25) The National Health Service is the most enduring aspect of Britain's post WWI welfare state, established in 1944.

Answer: TRUE
Page Ref: 329
Topic: Factual

26) What are five major components of medical services in the United States? Give an example of each.

Answer: These components include: physicians in solo practice; group outpatient settings, including groups of physicians sharing facilities; hospitals; public health services; sundry and corollary health services.
Page Ref: 304
Topic: Applied

27) List the four parts of the modern Medicare system.

Answer: These four parts include: compulsory Hospital insurance (Part A); Supplemental Medical Insurance (Part B); Medicare Advantage program (Part C); and the Medicare Prescription Drug, Improvement, and Modernization Act of 2003 (Part D).
Page Ref: 304
Topic: Factual

28) Under Medicare Part D, or MMA, to what does the "doughnut hole" refer?

Answer: This phrase refers to the fact that beneficiaries pay only 25% of total drug costs between $250 and $2,250. After reaching $2,250, the coverage ends and the beneficiary must pay the next $2,850 out–of–pocket.

Page Ref: 305
Topic: Applied

29) What do critics of Medicare Part D, or MMA, say in regard to its effectiveness?

Answer: The primary argument against MMA is that it does nothing to curb skyrocketing drug costs. In fact, MMA prohibits Medicare from negotiating lower prices.

Page Ref: 305
Topic: Conceptual

30) What are HSAs and what are they designed to accomplish?

Answer: HSAs are Health Savings Accounts and they are designed to offer a tax shelter to those with high deductible insurance. It is estimated that this component would cost the federal government $6.4 billion over the next decade. These accounts allow participants to put in money and withdraw it without being taxed. These accounts are very controversial among conservatives and liberals, because of cost and the population that the HSAs are most likely to serve, the rich and healthy.

Page Ref: 306
Topic: Conceptual

31) To what does "Medigap" insurance refer and why might it be necessary?

Answer: Medigap insurance refers to private insurance plans that pay most of the charges not covered by Medicare.

Page Ref: 307
Topic: Applied

32) What are the main differences between Medicare and Medicaid. In addition to programatically defining these programs, write a one sentence operational definition of each.

Answer: Pages 304–311 discuss the basic differences between these two programs. Students should be able to determine the population served by each of these programs and how they are financed.

Page Ref: 309
Topic: Applied

33) What are the three options given to states by the S–CHIP program in regard to covering uninsured children?

Answer: The options given to states in regard to S–CHIP are: the ability to design a new children's health insurance program; expanding current Medicaid programs, or a combination of both of the options.

Page Ref: 311
Topic: Conceptual

34) Discuss at least three tenets of the 1998 tobacco settlement.

Answer: The 1998 tobacco settlement established the following mandates: prohibition of youth targeting in advertising and promotion and other advertising limits; companies must develop corporate principles such as how to reduce youth smoking and appointing an executive to study Master Settlement Agreement mandates in relation to youth smoking; disbanding of tobacco trade organizations; limiting of industry lobbying funds; creates a $1.45 billion public education campaign.

Page Ref: 312
Topic: Factual

35) Does the U.S. health care system perform as well as other industrialized countries? Why or why not?

Answer: A majority of information points to the fact that the U.S. does NOT do as well in health care coverage of its citizens as do other industrialized countries. Information supporting this contingency is included on page 315 & 316.

Page Ref: 315
Topic: Applied

36) Explain at least three reasons why health care costs are so high in the U.S.

Answer: Some reasons mentioned in the text include: medical malpractice suits, treatment of people with AIDS, cost for development of innovative medical technology, cost to process insurance claims, longer life expectancy and cost to treat illnesses and diseases associated with the elderly.

Page Ref: 316
Topic: Applied

37) Discuss the role of the pharmaceutical industry in the rising cost of health care.

Answer: An extensive discussion of the industry's role in rising health care costs is included on page 318.

Page Ref: 318
Topic: Conceptual

38) What are the two aspects to cutting health care costs?

Answer: The first aspect to cutting health care costs is to cut the cost of governmental health care programs; the second involves lowering overall medical costs. Students should be able to expound on the impact of this two-fold cost-cutting ideology.

Page Ref: 318
Topic: Applied

39) Define managed care and discuss its various components. Evaluate the way in which managed care is shaping U.S. health care policy.

Answer: Managed care is defined as "an umbrella for health care insurance systems that contract with a network of hospitals, clinics, and doctors who agree to accept fees for each service or flat payments per patient. The advantage to providers is that they are given a ready source of referrals. Managed care inevitably shapes U.S. health care policy, because of the fact that 92% of providers (doctors) are involved in some way with a managed health care plan.

Page Ref: 319
Topic: Applied

40) Discuss at least two criticisms of managed care, particularly HMOs.

Answer: Quality of care is not as efficient or good, access to specialists is difficult for consumers, greater bureaucratization and impersonality, and other problems are said to plague managed care, particularly HMOs.

Page Ref: 320
Topic: Conceptual

Chapter 13   Mental Health and Substance Abuse Policy

1) To which of the following does "moral treatment" refer?

   A) Offering good air, clean water, food and activities to residents of mental health treatment facilities.

   B) Treatment of patients according to the Bible and Judeo–Christian principles.

   C) Offering educational opportunities affiliated with local religious organizations to encourage patients to adopt a certain faith base

   D) None of the above.

Answer: A
Page Ref: 338
Topic: Factual

2) In which of the following states did a majority of involuntary sterilizations and approximately how many were performed between 1930 & 1935?

   A) Michigan; 10,000

   B) New York; 25,000

   C) California; 20,000

   D) Involuntary sterilizations were not ever legal, any instances of this were considered "back alley" procedures.

Answer: C
Page Ref: 339
Topic: Factual

3) How many draftees were rejected for military service because of perceived mental illness during World War II?

   A) 50%   B) None   C) 10%   D) 25%

Answer: D
Page Ref: 340
Topic: Factual

4) What law enabled NIMH to reform mental health care provision?

   A) Mental Health Act of 1946

   B) Community Mental Health Centers Act of 1963

   C) Buck v. Bell

   D) Community Health Care Act of 1985

Answer: B
Page Ref: 340
Topic: Factual

5) What does secondary prevention seek to do?

    A) Limit the disability associated with mental illness.

    B) Detect mental illness early and provide effective treatment.

    C) Eliminate the cause of mental illness.

    D) None of the above.

Answer: D
Page Ref: 341
Topic: Factual

6) What does primary prevention seek to do?

    A) Limit the disability associated with mental illness.

    B) Detect mental illness early and provide effective treatment.

    C) Eliminate the cause of mental illness.

    D) Provide mental health services through primary care physicians.

Answer: C
Page Ref: 341
Topic: Factual

7) What does tertiary prevention seek to do?

    A) Limit the disability associated with mental illness.

    B) Detect mental illness early and provide effective treatment.'

    C) Eliminate the cause of mental illness.

    D) Provide services to minority populations.

Answer: A
Page Ref: 341
Topic: Factual

8) In Chapter 13, the authors refer to a "catchment area." What does this phrase conceptualize?

    A) a geographic definition of where CMHCs are to be located

    B) a political definition of where CMHCs are to be located

    C) a demographic definition of where CMHCs are to be located

    D) political sides regarding substance abuse policy

Answer: C
Page Ref: 341
Topic: Factual

9) Which presidential administration initially impounded funds appropriated for mental health programs, specifically CMHCs?

    A) Kennedy   B) Johnson   C) Nixon   D) Reagan

Answer: C
Page Ref: 341
Topic: Factual

10) What court decision contended that patients deserve treatment in the "least restrictive alternative?"

    A) Wyatt v. Stickney   B) Donaldson v. O' Connor

    C) Halderman v. Pennhurst   D) Buck v. Bell

Answer: C
Page Ref: 342
Topic: Factual

11) The most widely abused drug in the United States excluding tobacco is

    A) marijuana.   B) heroin.   C) alcohol.   D) cocaine.

Answer: C
Page Ref: 351
Topic: Factual

12) In what U.S. age population category has drug abuse increased slightly every year since 1997?

    A) 12–17   B) 18–25   C) 26–35   D) 55+

Answer: B
Page Ref: 354
Topic: Factual

13) Of all the treatment episodes involving alcohol and drugs, those involving alcohol represent what percent?

    A) 15   B) 25   C) 50   D) 75

Answer: C
Page Ref: 356
Topic: Factual

14) Since 1993, the number of treatment episodes has grown fastest for which substance?

    A) marijuana   B) heroin   C) alcohol   D) cocaine

Answer: A
Page Ref: 356
Topic: Factual

15) The fastest growing auspice in which NASW members work is

    A) public.   B) private non-profit.

    C) private for profit.   D) health care.

Answer: C
Page Ref: 357
Topic: Factual

16) Before the rise of the community mental health movement, the federal government was solely responsible for the care of the mentaly ill.

Answer: FALSE
Page Ref: 338
Topic: Applied

17) Institutional care for the chronically mentally ill has been proven as the superior method of treatment since the early 1960s.

Answer: FALSE
Page Ref: 340
Topic: Applied

18) The Community Mental Health Centers Act of 1963 provided funds for service delivery and construction of new mental health care facilities.

Answer: FALSE
Page Ref: 340
Topic: Applied

19) State hospitals of the early 1960s primarily addressed primary prevention.

Answer: FALSE
Page Ref: 341
Topic: Conceptual

20) Community mental health focus combining primary and secondary intervention.

Answer: TRUE
Page Ref: 341
Topic: Factual

21) Deinstitutionalization received little support when first instituted.

Answer: FALSE
Page Ref: 341
Topic: Applied

22) As a result of deinstitutionalization and CMHCs, the recidivism rate for hospitalized mentally ill patients has dramatically increased.

Answer: TRUE
Page Ref: 341
Topic: Factual

23) A majority of institutionalized mentally ill patients die as a result of suicide.

Answer: FALSE
Page Ref: 342
Topic: Factual

24) The Reagan administration's drug policy emphasized treatment and public education.

Answer: FALSE
Page Ref: 354
Topic: Factual

25) ESOP's are a kind of EAP.

Answer: FALSE
Page Ref: 362
Topic: Factual

26) What did the passage of the Mental Health Parity Act establish for the mentally ill? What are the ramifications of this act's passage?

Answer: This act mandated that employers offer employees mental health benefits that were comparable to physical health care benefits.
Page Ref: 338
Topic: Conceptual

27) Who was Dorthea Dix and for what is she known?

Answer: Dorthea Dix was a social worker best known for her activity in the 1840s that convinced many states to construct special institutions to provide asylum to the emotionally deranged. Congress heard Ms. Dix's message and thereby passed legislation authorizing federal aid to the states for mental institutions.
Page Ref: 338
Topic: Conceptual

28) What did the 1927 Supreme Court decision in Buck v. Bell establish? How was this decision important to the cause of protecting our nation's mentally ill?

Answer: This court case validated the practice of involuntary sterilization. Student answers will vary, but should include comment regarding the fact that this court decision was a set-back in the freedom protection of the mentally ill.
Page Ref: 339
Topic: Conceptual

29) What was the Eugenics Movement?

Answer: The Eugenics Movement provided a straightforward and precise surgical solution to the problem of state institution overcrowding — sterilizing those who are mentally ill.
Page Ref: 339
Topic: Conceptual

30) Discuss the four reasons why the NIMH's Action for Mental Health was considered idealistic?

Answer: 1) The postwar economy was booming and the lack of need for military protection created a surplus for domestic issues; 2) Psychotropic medications were beginning to emerge as effective treatment for the mentally ill; 3) Literature criticized institutionalization and lauded the benefits of community care; and 4) President John F. Kennedy, because of personal family experience with mental retardation, was supportive of programming designed to improve mental health care.

Page Ref: 340
Topic: Conceptual

31) Programmatically, what were community health centers designed to provide?

Answer: CHCs were programmed to provide all essential psychiatric services, including hospitalization, outpatient services, 24-hour emergency services, and consultation and education for other service providers in the community. Soon after they were initially founded, CHCs included child mental health, as well as substance abuse issues services.

Page Ref: 341
Topic: Conceptual

32) What does taking a "case management" approach to mental health care mean?

Answer: This approach is set-up so that each case is assigned to one professional who monitors the patient's progress toward treatment.

Page Ref: 341
Topic: Conceptual

33) What did the Omnibus Budget and Reconciliation Act of 1981 do to mental health funding?

Answer: The OBRA, pushed through during the Reagan administration, collapsed all mental health funding into a block grant available to states for any mental health services they deemed fundable. As a direct result, the designation of CMHCs for direct receipt of federal funds ceased in 1981.

Page Ref: 341
Topic: Conceptual

34) How has deinstitutionalization marginalized the mentally ill?

Answer: This essay question is very broad and while answers will vary and include various opinions regarding the plight of the mentally ill, students should answer in line with information found on pages 13–14 through 13–15.

Page Ref: 341
Topic: Conceptual

35) How has the evolution of psychotropic medications affected the plight of the mentally ill?

Answer: Psychotropic medications are a "mixed bag." On one hand, they stabilize some patients in ways that only hospitalization or therapy could not. On the other hand, they create unwanted side effects and are relied on as a primary treatment modality.

Page Ref: 344
Topic: Conceptual

36) Discuss the incidence of mental illness in the correctional system.

Answer: Answers will vary regarding this question, but should address the fact that the correctional system is often used as a place for psychiatric patients to be "housed." One organization reports that there are three times as many psychiatric patients in jails as there are in hospitals and the gap is continuing to widen.

Page Ref: 344
Topic: Applied

37) Discuss the pros and cons of a focus on preventative commitments for our society's mentally ill.

Answer: Answers will vary, but students should show a grasp of the fact that this is a widely debated topic and one that appears to be increasing in popularity amongst mental health care providers.

Page Ref: 346
Topic: Conceptual

38) What is capitation and how does it affect service delivery for mental health services?

Answer: Capitation is a set amount of money per patient that is used to provide a wide array of physical and mental health services. While this method often produces a cost savings, it can also affect the quality of care given patients in this kind of system.

Page Ref: 347
Topic: Conceptual

39) What has the federal government's two-fold response been to illicit drug use?

Answer: The current policies involve interdicting the supply of illegal substances and reducing the demand through treatment and education.

Page Ref: 354
Topic: Factual

40) What is the YAVIS syndrome and to what phenomena does it apply?

Answer: YAVIS stands for "young, attractive, verbal, intelligent, and successful" and applies to the population that tends to represent the clientele of private practitioners.

Page Ref: 359
Topic: Conceptual

Chapter 14 Criminal Justice

1) Modern criminology dates from

    A) the Enlightenment era.   B) the Renaissance Period.

    C) the Progressive era of social work.   D) American Colonial period.

Answer: A
Page Ref: 369
Topic: Factual

2) In the early to mid–1800s which of the following did not contribute to the lack of support for humane institutions?

    A) Dorothea Dix and her reform movement

    B) the American ethos of rugged individualism

    C) an influx of immigrants many of whom became institutionalized

    D) the Pierce veto in 1854

Answer: A
Page Ref: 369
Topic: Conceptual

3) Cesare Beccaria applied all BUT WHICH of the following philosophies to corrections in the early history of the U.S.?

    A) Rehabilitation of criminals is key to prevent recidivism.

    B) Crime can be measured by its severity.

    C) Incarceration should segregate prisoners.

    D) The purpose of punishment is deterrence.

Answer: A
Page Ref: 369
Topic: Conceptual

4) On average, how much does imprisonment cost per inmate every year?

    A) $53,000   B) $15,000   C) $7,500   D) $22,000

Answer: D
Page Ref: 370
Topic: Factual

5) Which of the following categories steadily increased in number between 1989 & 2000?

    A) number of adults on probation   B) number of adults on parole

    C) number of adults in jail   D) all of the above

Answer: D
Page Ref: 372
Topic: Conceptual

6) Which of the following is a characteristic of the criminal justice system in the United States?

  A) Despite privatization, the federal government maintains a majority of prisons in the U.S.

  B) The incarceration rate of the U.S. is second only to Russia.

  C) The federal government outspends the states in costs relating to incarceration.

  D) There is agreement by experts as to the reasons why there are increases/decreases in crime.

Answer: B
Page Ref: 372
Topic: Applied

7) Which of the following statements reflect the criminal justice systems' thinking relative to developing programming for juveniles?

  A) The majority of adult offenders were also known to the juvenile justice system.

  B) Young deviants are good candidates for becoming adult deviants.

  C) From a prevention standpoint reaching youngsters early is important.

  D) all of the above

Answer: D
Page Ref: 373
Topic: Applied

8) Which statement below does NOT accurately describe boot camps for juveniles?

  A) At boot camps, inmates would receive physical training and military discipline.

  B) By 1993, boot camps had been established in 25 states.

  C) A boot camp in Connecticut experienced gang activity, sexual activity and gambling.

  D) An analysis of boot camps concluded that alumni were less likely to commit future offenses.

Answer: D
Page Ref: 374
Topic: Conceptual

9) In 2000, a majority of juvenile offenders were arrested for

  A) robbery.   B) drug sales.

  C) assault.   D) drug possession.

Answer: D
Page Ref: 374
Topic: Factual

10) Which statement below does NOT accurately reflect the War on Drugs in the 1980s?

   A) Interdiction efforts have proven to be exceptionally successful.

   B) Funding for prevention and treatment lagged far behind allocations for incarceration.

   C) By 1997, drug abuse accounted for more arrests than any other offense

   D) None of the above.

Answer: A
Page Ref: 376
Topic: Applied

11) What percentage of African Americans between the ages of 20–29 were incarcerated, on parole, or on probation?

   A) 10   B) 25   C) 42   D) 5

Answer: B
Page Ref: 378
Topic: Factual

12) Authors Bennett and Dilulio cited behavior of prisoners on parole committing crimes as examples of

   A) need for more community–based programs.

   B) successful drug interdiction making illegal substances more scarce.

   C) moral poverty.

   D) case work being ineffective.

Answer: C
Page Ref: 379
Topic: Conceptual

13) Which statement is NOT related to the concept of "social embeddedness"?

   A) The presence of an adult offender in a family does not increase the likelihood of children in that family entering the juvenile justice system.

   B) There are environmental influences in criminal conduct.

   C) Criminal arrests label youngsters and disrupt education and employment.

   D) Contacts with criminal friends are more likely to integrate youths into the criminal underworld.

Answer: A
Page Ref: 380
Topic: Conceptual

14) Which of the statements below are used to support the argument for the legalization of drugs?

A) Destigmatization of drug abuse could mean more drug abusers entering treatment.

B) By legalizing drugs, substantial sums of money would be freed from law enforcement activity and could be channeled to prevention services.

C) Prison populations would be cut significantly.

D) all of the above

Answer: D
Page Ref: 381
Topic: Conceptual

15) Which of the statements below is not associated with the concept of "new penology"?

A) The U.S. Sentencing Commission established the same prison sentence for the use of crack and for the use of cocaine.

B) The mission of criminal justice became "rabble management."

C) In 1994, the Violent Crime Control and Law Enforcement Act introduced the "three strikes" penalties for repeat offenders.

D) In little more than a decade the number of prisoners under the death sentence had tripled.

Answer: A
Page Ref: 382
Topic: Conceptual

16) John Augustus is known as the initiator of what is now our contemporary form of probation.

Answer: TRUE
Page Ref: 369
Topic: Factual

17) The federal government provides a significantly larger portion of criminal justice services than state and local governments.

Answer: FALSE
Page Ref: 369
Topic: Conceptual

18) During the 1990s, all categories of crime increased slightly.

Answer: FALSE
Page Ref: 371
Topic: Applied

19) In 2000 there were almost 2 million adults in jail or prison in the U.S.

Answer: TRUE
Page Ref: 372
Topic: Factual

20) The first institution for juvenile delinquency was Charles Loring Brace's New York Children's Aid Society, established in 1853.

Answer: FALSE
Page Ref: 373
Topic: Factual

21) Boot camps have been empirically proven to offer successful treatment and intervention for juvenile offenders.

Answer: FALSE
Page Ref: 374
Topic: Conceptual

22) Incarceration is the "intervention of choice" for youth offenders.

Answer: TRUE
Page Ref: 374
Topic: Factual

23) Because of the War on Drugs in the 1980s, funds for law enforcement decreased, while funds for prevention, education, and treatment increased.

Answer: FALSE
Page Ref: 375
Topic: Factual

24) Despite unrelenting efforts to contain drug abuse and keep individuals from using drugs, there was an increased number of drug seizures, growing fourfold between 1999 and 2000.

Answer: TRUE
Page Ref: 375
Topic: Applied

25) Should the War on Drugs continue as it is now, cost savings could be near $100 billion over the next 20 years.

Answer: FALSE
Page Ref: 375
Topic: Conceptual

26) What is the reasoning given for the 1990s drop in crime?

Answer: The reasons, however unclear, are that younger, more crime-prone people are aging and less likely to be violent, crime policies. Additionally, it is postulated that the actual crime figures may be may be flawed, depending on whether or not you are looking at the FBI's or the Nation Crime Survey's results.
Page Ref: 370
Topic: Applied

27) Discuss the gender and racial trends for incarcerated persons.

Answer: Approximately 90% of inmates are men, 2/3 are minorities of color. Half are African American. In 2002, 12% of black men between the ages of 20-34 were behind bars. Approximately 2/3 of inmates return to prison within a few years of release, making recidivism an enormous burden on the AA community.

Page Ref: 373
Topic: Conceptual

28) Did Jerome Miller feel that the 1972 Juvenile Justice and Delinquency Prevention Act was successful? Why or why not?

Answer: Mr. Miller stated that the act "failed miserably." He was so discouraged by the act's lack of effectiveness at the Department of Youth Services, that he discharged many of the youth in his care as Executive Director and closed down DYS operations.

Page Ref: 373
Topic: Conceptual

29) Discuss the two strategies that dominated the "War on Drugs."

Answer: The WOD focused on government interdiction to eliminate the substance & treatment programs to diminish the need for illegal drugs. Students should be able to expound on these two foci.

Page Ref: 375
Topic: Conceptual

30) What are the goals of the Office of National Drug Control Policy (ONDCP)?

Answer: The ONDCP sets policies, priorities, and objectives for the nation's drug control program. The goals of the program are to reduce illicit drug use, manufacturing, trafficking, drug related crime, and violence and health-related drug consequences.

Page Ref: 376
Topic: Conceptual

31) Jerome Miller asserted that prisons are something of a "simple internment camp" for minority youth. What are the assumptions behind this claim? Do you agree or disagree?

Answer: Student answers will vary, but should include the fact that prisons hold a large number of minority populations (some estimates are as high as 25% of African Americans 20-29 years old) vs. majority populations.

Page Ref: 379
Topic: Conceptual

32) What is "moral poverty?"

Answer: Moral poverty is a phrase coined by William Bennett, John DiIulio, Jr. and John Walters in their BODY COUNT, which stated that it was truly the poverty of being without loving adults, role models, growing up severely abused, neglected, etc. at the hands of a deviant adult.

Page Ref: 379
Topic: Conceptual

33) Do you believe, as does William Julius Wilson, that "lawlessness declines as rates of employment and marriage rise?" Why or why not?

Answer: Student answers will vary.
Page Ref: 381
Topic: Conceptual

34) What reasons do proponents of drug legalization give for the policy's implementation?

Answer: 1) individuals should be free to engage in any activity, as long as it does not harm others; 2) noting massive sums of money pumped into law enforcement and meager treatment and interdiction results - similar to Prohibition legislation; 3) easier to regulate substances as we do with alcohol and tobacco, with some sort of tax; 4) free up large sums of money for enforcement and place it toward abuse prevention and treatment; 5) decriminalize drug use, cutting prison population significantly; and 6) destigmatize drugs, causing folks to possibly be more apt to seek treatment
Page Ref: 381
Topic: Conceptual

35) What reasons are against the legalization of illicit drugs?

Answer: 1) logistics-which drugs will be legal, which ones illegal; 2) should availability be unlimited and should age restrictions apply? ; 3) taxation would still force the government to maintain a tax code, regulate product safety, and maintain a taxing authority; 4) influx of crack cocaine as being a drug that "didn't just affect the person using the drug"
Page Ref: 381
Topic: Conceptual

36) What did 1994's Violent Crime Control and Law Enforcement Act do?

Answer: It introduced the "three strikes" penalty for repeat offenders and increased the # of federal crimes to which the death penalty applied.
Page Ref: 382
Topic: Conceptual

37) To what does the term "new penology" refer? How is it different than the "old penology?"

Answer: The rapid expansion in correctional facilities resulting in efficient management of large populations of high-risk offenders. The mission became "managerial, not transformative." Old penology focused on individual rehab (via parole or probation) or deterrence (via incarceration).
Page Ref: 383
Topic: Conceptual

38) What makes up the "iron triangle" of the prison-industrial complex?

Answer: The "iron triangle" consists of government bureaucrats, private industry leaders, and politicians who work together to expand the criminal justice system.
Page Ref: 383
Topic: Conceptual

39) What is "community policing" and why is it effective?

   Answer: This program, conceived in Houston reassigns law enforcement offices from patrol cars and specialty units to beats on the streets of high-crime areas.
   Page Ref: 384
   Topic: Applied

40) Discuss issues surrounding death sentence review for the mentally retarded.

   Answer: It has been estimated that approximately 10% of the inmates on death row are mentally retarded, although this status is recognized by only 13 of the 38 states permitting capital punishments. In 2002, the Supreme Court ruled that executing retarded inmates was unconstitutional.
   Page Ref: 385
   Topic: Conceptual

Chapter 15   Child Welfare Policy

1) The percent of children in poverty in the United States (1996):

   A) 12   B) 8   C) 16   D) 22

Answer: D
Page Ref: 390
Topic: Factual

2) In 2002, how many children were living in poverty?

   A) 5 million   B) 600,000   C) 10 million   D) 12 million

Answer: D
Page Ref: 390
Topic: Factual

3) Which of the following is NOT one of the major components of child welfare programs?

   A) Food Stamps   B) Adoption

   C) Foster Care   D) Child Protective Services

Answer: A
Page Ref: 391
Topic: Applied

4) Who founded the New York Children's Aid Society?

   A) James West   B) Etta Wheeler

   C) Dorthea Dix   D) Charles Loring Brace

Answer: D
Page Ref: 392
Topic: Factual

5) Which of the following acts established programs decreasing the nation's infant mortality rate?

   A) The Healthy Mothers Happy Babies Act of 1935

   B) The Child Labor Act of 1916

   C) The Maternity and Infancy Act of 1921

   D) The Children's Bureau Act of 1912

Answer: C
Page Ref: 392
Topic: Factual

6) Which of the following served as a precursor to Aid to Dependent Children in 1935?

   A) Aid to Families with Dependent Children

   B) Aid to Destitute Families

   C) Funds for Parents Act

   D) Temporary Assistance to Needy Families

   Answer: C
   Page Ref: 393
   Topic: Factual

7) Douglas Besharov contends that 1,000 children die under circumstances suggestive of parental maltreatment each year. What percentage of these cases were previously reported?

   A) 50%   B) 75%

   C) 20%   D) none of the above

   Answer: A
   Page Ref: 394
   Topic: Factual

8) The CAPTA legislation was enacted about how many years after the founding of the New York Society for the Prevention of Cruelty to Children?

   A) 50   B) 100   C) that same year   D) 75

   Answer: B
   Page Ref: 394
   Topic: Factual

9) Between 1993 and 2001, how many children died as a result of maltreatment in the District of Columbia?

   A) 229   B) 51   C) 72   D) 396

   Answer: A
   Page Ref: 396
   Topic: Factual

10) According to the U.S. Advisory Commission on Child Abuse and Neglect, how many children die of abuse and neglect annually?

   A) 2,000   B) 800   C) 5,000   D) 10,000

   Answer: A
   Page Ref: 397
   Topic: Factual

11) The Child Welfare League of America suggests that caseloads for workers not exceed

   A) 100.   B) 25.   C) 17.   D) 55.

   Answer: C
   Page Ref: 397
   Topic: Factual

12) From 1976 to 1996, the number of maltreated children has

    A) dropped significantly.   B) tripled.

    C) quadrupled.   D) doubled.

Answer: C
Page Ref: 398
Topic: Factual

13) The largest part of federal funding for child welfare services is spent on

    A) Adoption.   B) Foster care.

    C) Independent living.   D) CPS.

Answer: B
Page Ref: 402
Topic: Factual

14) What was the percentage in 2001 of children who were reunited with their families following CPS investigation?

    A) 44   B) 75   C) 10   D) 25

Answer: A
Page Ref: 405
Topic: Factual

15) Which is the largest source of federal financial support for child care?

    A) Child Care Tax Credit

    B) Child Care and Child Development Block Grant

    C) Title XX

    D) Earned Income Tax Credit

Answer: A
Page Ref: 408
Topic: Factual

16) According to the Luxembourg Study, which rated the number of children in poverty, the United States ranked last.

Answer: TRUE
Page Ref: 390
Topic: Conceptual

17) In two out of five child abuse cases, workers ignored previous reports of child abuse to those victims.

Answer: TRUE
Page Ref: 395
Topic: Factual

18) High turnover among staff in public child protective agencies has been a problem over the past 15 years.

Answer: TRUE
Page Ref: 395
Topic: Factual

19) The New York Society for the Prevention of Cruelty to Animals existed before the New York Society for the Prevention of Cruelty to Children.

Answer: TRUE
Page Ref: 392
Topic: Applied

20) The Social Security Act of 1935 created major new programs to provide child welfare services.

Answer: FALSE
Page Ref: 393
Topic: Factual

21) The number of child maltreatment cases is greater among girls than boys.

Answer: TRUE
Page Ref: 393
Topic: Factual

22) The majority of maltreatment cases involve African-American children.

Answer: FALSE
Page Ref: 393
Topic: Factual

23) African-American children are disproportionately represented in child maltreatment cases.

Answer: TRUE
Page Ref: 398
Topic: Factual

24) Head Start Funding has grown substantially since 1980.

Answer: TRUE
Page Ref: 407
Topic: Factual

25) Current funding for Head Start is adequate for serving most eligible children.

Answer: FALSE
Page Ref: 407
Topic: Conceptual

26) Why are child welfare services often controversial?

Answer: Because they sanction the intervention of human service professionals in family affairs that are ordinarily assumed to be private matters and prerogative of parents.

Page Ref: 391
Topic: Conceptual

27) What incident sparked the genesis of protective services for children in the United States?

Answer: Etta Wheeler, in 1874, discovered that a nine year–old child, Mary Ellen, was tied to a bed, being whipped, and stabbed with scissors. Ms. Wheeler spoke with the director of the New York SPCA and had Mary Ellen removed from her home based on laws in place at the time for handling cases of abused and battered children.

Page Ref: 392
Topic: Conceptual

28) What was the dual strategy of the National Consumer League regarding advocacy for women and children?

Answer: First, the League lobbied for reform in the working conditions of women through regulation of sweatshops and factories, and for ending the exploitation of children by prohibiting child labor. Second, it advocated ameliorating the grinding poverty of many families by means of a family subsidy that would make such deplorable work less necessary.

Page Ref: 393
Topic: Applied

29) How did the Social Security Act of 1935 address child welfare?

Answer: In two of its provisions, the SSA addressed child welfare. Title IV introduced the Aid to Dependent Children, which provided public relief to needy children through cash grants to their families. Title V reestablished Maternal and Child Welfare Services (expired in 1929) and expanded the mandate of the Children's Bureau, whose goal was now to oversee a new set of child welfare services "for the protection and care of homeless, dependent, and neglected children, and children in danger of becoming delinquent."

Page Ref: 393
Topic: Conceptual

30) What were the four major specifications of the Child Abuse Prevention and Treatment Act of 1974?

Answer: The four major specifications were: 1) a standard definition of child abuse; 2) methods for reporting and investigating abuse and neglect; 3) immunity for those reporting suspected injuries inflicted on children; 4) prevention and public education efforts to reduce the incidents of abuse and neglect.

Page Ref: 394
Topic: Conceptual

31) To what does the term "family preservation" refer?

Answer: This ideology called for the provision of intensive services for a brief period, all intended to stabilize the family and prevent out-of-home placement of a child.
Page Ref: 397
Topic: Applied

32) Discuss the findings of the 2003 Administration on Children and Families in regard to States' outcomes. Overall, was this report promising or discouraging regarding child welfare?

Answer: Unfortunately, the report documented that a majority of states failed to be in compliance on every outcome measure. On two outcomes, not one state was in "substantial conformity."
Page Ref: 399
Topic: Conceptual

33) What did the Annie E. Casey Foundation identify as a significant impediment to progress in regard to child welfare? Why?

Answer: The Foundation identified the human services workforce as "reaching a state of crisis." Excerpts from this report can be found on page 401.
Page Ref: 401
Topic: Applied

34) What was a central feature of the Adoption Assistance and Child Welfare Act of 1980 and what does this concept entail?

Answer: Permanency planning became a central feature of the AACWA. This feature is defined as "the systematic process of carrying out, within a brief time-limited period, a set of goal-directed activities designed to help children live in families that offer continuity of relationships with nurturing parents or caretakers and the opportunity to establish lifetime relationships.
Page Ref: 402
Topic: Conceptual

35) Should agencies give consideration to maintaining the cultural identity of children placed for adoption by finding them homes in their birth culture?

Answer: Answers to this question will vary.
Page Ref: 405
Topic: Conceptual

36) What did the Indian Child Welfare Act do?

Answer: This act established tribes, rather than state courts, as the governing bodies responsible for Indian foster children.
Page Ref: 405
Topic: Conceptual

37) What are the primary programs assisting parents with child care expenses?

Answer: The primary programs are: the federal dependent care tax credit, the child care tax credit, the Child Care and Development Block Grant, and Title XX.

Page Ref: 408
Topic: Conceptual

38) What is the primary federal program established for provision to low income pregnant women? What does it provide?

Answer: WIC, the Special Supplemental Nutrition Program for Women, Infants and Children provides such services. Low-income pregnant women and nursing women receive food coupons.

Page Ref: 409
Topic: Conceptual

39) Why does childbearing among very young unmarried women pose a serious problem for public policy?

Answer: First teenage mothers are more likely to drop out of school and thus fail to gain skills that would make them self-sufficient. Second, teenage mothers are more likely to have to depend on welfare, the benefits of which are at levels lower than the actual cost of raising children.

Page Ref: 410
Topic: Conceptual

40) What do the authors conclude regarding the future of child welfare?

Answer: A detailed answer to this question can be found on pages 411 & 412. Students should be able to show a grasp of the basic conclusions made regarding child welfare.

Page Ref: 411
Topic: Conceptual

Chapter 16 Housing Policies

1) Which of the following statements is NOT accurate about the HOME program?

   A) HOME II finances public sale of living locales.

   B) 15% of HOME funds must be used for projects sponsored by Community Housing Development organizations.

   C) Matching funds cannot be used for new construction.

   D) HOME allows states some flexibility in addressing their housing needs.

   Answer: C
   Page Ref: 417
   Topic: Conceptual

2) The goal to create a United States Housing Authority was part of the

   A) Housing Act of 1949.

   B) Housing Act of 1937.

   C) Demonstration Cities and Metropolitan Development Act.

   D) Community Reinvestment Act.

   Answer: B
   Page Ref: 417
   Topic: Conceptual

3) Which of the below is NOT a goal of the Cranston–Gonzales National Affordable Housing Act?

   A) link housing assistance with social services

   B) centralize housing policy

   C) facilitate home ownership

   D) preserve existing federally subsidized housing units

   Answer: B
   Page Ref: 417
   Topic: Conceptual

4) What housing act cleared the way for massive slum clearance projects?

   A) Housing Act of 1954

   B) The Housing and Community Development Act of 1974

   C) Housing Act of 1949

   D) The Demonstration Cities and Metropolitan Development Act

   Answer: A
   Page Ref: 418
   Topic: Factual

5) Which of the statements about HUD Section 8 housing is NOT accurate?

   A) Section 8 is based on a voucher system.

   B) Three quarters of Section 8 is project-based.

   C) Low-income tenants can occupy existing and privately owned housing stock.

   D) Section 8 provides funds for new construction.

Answer: B
Page Ref: 421
Topic: Applied

6) Which of the following statements is NOT accurate regarding public housing programs?

   A) Federal housing programs were cut back in the 1980s and 1990s.

   B) Section 8 housing could be replaced by HANF.

   C) Waiting lists for housing can be as long as two or more years.

   D) One-half of poor renter households receive government subsidies.

Answer: D
Page Ref: 422
Topic: Applied

7) Senate Bill 947 ended the Housing Choice Voucher program. The potential replacement for this bill now being considered is

   A) Revitalization of Severely Distressed Public Housing.

   B) Brownfields Redevelopment.

   C) Government National Mortgage Association (Ginnie Mae).

   D) Housing Assistance for Needy Families.

Answer: D
Page Ref: 422
Topic: Factual

8) What percentage of Section 8 Housing households are families with children?

   A) 61   B) 87   C) 22   D) 43

Answer: A
Page Ref: 423
Topic: Factual

9) The national home ownership rate in 2003 was approximately:

   A) 35   B) 70   C) 15   D) 5

Answer: B
Page Ref: 424
Topic: Factual

10) The standard benchmark for "affordability" is that households should pay no more than what percentage of their income for housing?

   A) 30   B) 40   C) 20   D) 50

   Answer: A
   Page Ref: 428
   Topic: Factual

11) As a result of urban renewal projects which of the following statements is NOT accurate?

   A) "Gentrified" neighborhoods sprung up with affordable housing for low-income families.

   B) Many cheap single-room occupancy (SRO) hotels were razed leading to more homeless.

   C) Gentrification becomes a widespread phenomena.

   D) Localities tried to attract upper income families to revitalized inner cities often at the expense of poor families.

   Answer: A
   Page Ref: 429
   Topic: Conceptual

12) Which of the following statements does NOT accurately reflect the condition of the homeless in the United States?

   A) For some, homelessness is a life-style choice.

   B) Homelessness and poverty are not linked.

   C) Many in the homeless population suffer from a diagnosable mental illness or have substance abuse-related issues.

   D) The homeless population is often undercounted in federal surveys for political purposes.

   Answer: B
   Page Ref: 433
   Topic: Conceptual

13) What percentage of the homeless are children?

   A) 40   B) 30   C) 20   D) 10

   Answer: A
   Page Ref: 433
   Topic: Factual

14) What percentage of the homeless population is under the age of 24?

   A) 35   B) 5   C) 58   D) 14

   Answer: D
   Page Ref: 435
   Topic: Factual

15) Which of the following points are parts of Hartman's solution to end homelessness?

A) preserve the SRO hotels

B) provision of suitable residential alternatives for people with mental illness

C) establish a national "right to shelter"

D) all of the above

Answer: D
Page Ref: 436
Topic: Applied

16) The Cranston–Gonzales National Affordable Housing Act authorized housing-related block grants to state and local governments.

Answer: TRUE
Page Ref: 417
Topic: Applied

17) Ninety percent of HOME-assisted units in jurisdiction must be affordable for families with incomes below 60 percent of the area median, with the remaining units being affordable for families with incomes up to 80 percent of the median.

Answer: TRUE
Page Ref: 417
Topic: Factual

18) The Quality Housing and Work Responsibility Act of 1998 was the housing equivalent of the 1996 PRWOA.

Answer: TRUE
Page Ref: 417
Topic: Conceptual

19) For many families, the cost of housing represents the single largest expenditure in the household budget.

Answer: TRUE
Page Ref: 418
Topic: Conceptual

20) Public Housing was established by the U.S. Housing Act of 1937.

Answer: TRUE
Page Ref: 421
Topic: Factual

21) The Capital Grants program is interest-free, but requires repayment within 3 years.

Answer: FALSE
Page Ref: 421
Topic: Applied

22) Homeless Assistance Grants are designed to provide temporary, short-term housing for the homeless population.

Answer: FALSE
Page Ref: 422
Topic: Conceptual

23) According to the Joint Center for Housing Studies of Harvard University, only 10% of Americans list their home as their single biggest asset.

Answer: FALSE
Page Ref: 422
Topic: Factual

24) In 2004, the average cost of a new single family home in the U.S. was $263,000.

Answer: TRUE
Page Ref: 425
Topic: Factual

25) More than 40% of the homeless population reports being sexually assaulted while on the streets.

Answer: FALSE
Page Ref: 433
Topic: Factual

26) What were the goals of the Cranston-Gonzales National Affordable Housing Act?

Answer: The goals included: 1) decentralizing housing policy by allowing states to design and administer their own housing programs; 2) using nonprofit sponsors to help develop and implement housing services; 3) linking housing assistance more closely with social services; 4) facilitating home ownership for low and moderate income people; 5) preserving existing federally subsidized housing units; and 6)initiating cost sharing among federal, state and local governments and nonprofit organizations.
Page Ref: 417
Topic: Conceptual

27) How does the Quality Housing and Work Responsibility Act of 1998 tie workforce participation into housing benefits?

Answer: A detailed discussion of the links between the QHWRA and workforce participation are found on pages 417–418.
Topic: Conceptual

28) What are the four components of the Homeownership and Opportunity for People Everywhere program?

Answer: HOPE has four components, as it: 1) finances the sale of public housing apartments to residents; 2) finances the sales to low-income persons of other apartment buildings held by the federal government; 3) finances the sale of single-family homes owned by the federal, state of local governments; and 4) represents an effort to combine social services with housing assistance for elderly and disabled households that would otherwise be unable to live independently.

Page Ref: 417
Topic: Conceptual

29) Discuss at least 3 of the historical highlights of housing legislation.

Answer: Figure 16.1 on page 418 addresses 7 acts of legislation that significantly impacted housing in the U.S. from 1937-1974, and currently.

Page Ref: 418
Topic: Applied

30) What is the Low Income Housing Tax Credit and what does it seek to do?

Answer: The LIHTC was a way for the federal government to encourage the development of affordable housing without having to allocate direct federal expenditures.

Page Ref: 418
Topic: Applied

31) What is "redlining" in regard to housing policy?

Answer: Redlining is defined as "an outright refusal of an insurance company, bank or other financial institution to provide its services solely on the basis of the location of a property.

Page Ref: 418
Topic: Applied

32) What factors affect housing affordability for low-income home owners?

Answer: Many factors affecting housing affordability are discussed in detail on pages 425 & 426. Students should be able to demonstrate understanding of the issues facing low-income homeowners and inevitably, the rising cost of homes, coupled with excruciatingly high mortgage rates in the fringe economy are "bare bones" requirements for this question's answer.

Page Ref: 425
Topic: Conceptual

33) Is there evidence that a crisis in affordable rental housing exists? Cite examples in support of your answer.

Answer: A detailed discussion of findings in this area can be found on page 428. Please review these specifics before determining what quality of answer you will require from your students.

Page Ref: 428
Topic: Applied

34) What is a circuit breaker program?

Answer: A CBP is the most common form of property tax relief. A typical program is activated when taxes exceed a specified proportion of a homeowner's income, and in some states, low income households are sent a yearly benefit check that covers all or part of the property taxes they paid.

Page Ref: 430
Topic: Applied

35) Why is the actual number of homeless people in the United States difficult to ascertain?

Answer: First, definitions of homelessness vary from study to study, and different methods for counting homeless yield different results. Second, many of the homeless are "hidden" in that they live in campgrounds, automobiles, boxcars, caves, tents, etc. Or, they may live temporarily with family members or friends.

Page Ref: 431
Topic: Applied

36) What seems to indicate greater chronicity and length of homelessness?

Answer: The answer to this question can be found, discussed in great detail on pages 434 & 435.
Page Ref: 434
Topic: Conceptual

37) Have there been attempts to address homelessness? Have these attempts been successful? Name and discuss at least two provisions by the federal government.

Answer: Pages 435 & 436 contain a bevy of information addressing the government's attempts to address homelessness, including grants, programs, and shelter accommodations.
Page Ref: 435
Topic: Applied

38) What is Chester Hartman's nine-point proposal for putting an end to homelessness?

Answer: Mr. Hartman suggests the following nine tenets: 1) increase the number of new and rehabilitated units offered to lower-income households; 2) lower the required rent/income ratio in government housing from 30-25%; 3) arrest the depletion of low-income housing through neglect, abandonment, conversion, and sale; 4) preserve the SRO hotels; 5) establish a national "right to shelter"; 6) require local governments to make available properties that can used as shelters and second stage housing; 7) create legislation that gives tenants reasonable protection from eviction; 8) provide governmental assistance to homeowners facing foreclosure; 9) provide suitable residential alternatives for mentally ill persons.

Page Ref: 436
Topic: Conceptual

39) What are two recommendations given for housing reform that you perceive as viable solutions? Why?

Answer: Students may choose from numerous recommendations made by the authors on pages 437-439.
Page Ref: 437
Topic: Conceptual

40) Discuss the housing crisis in terms of availability and affordability.

Answer: Answers will vary, but students should demonstrate a grasp of the enormity of the situation in this country, as discussed throughout the chapter.

Page Ref: 438
Topic: Applied

Chapter 17 The Policies of Food Policy and Rural Life

1) Which of the following statements does NOT accurately describe conditions in the United States?

   A) Undernourished children are at high-risk for becoming poor performers in school.

   B) Americans spend a smaller percentage of their income on food than any other nation.

   C) One-quarter of U.S. food stock is thrown away.

   D) Three percent of American households either suffer from hunger or worry about going hungry.

   Answer: D
   Page Ref: 443
   Topic: Conceptual

2) Over the course of a year, what percentage of Americans participate in a food assistance program?

   A) 10   B) 15   C) 20   D) 5

   Answer: C
   Page Ref: 443
   Topic: Factual

3) U. S. food policy

   A) is almost completely subsidized.

   B) is based on the belief that the government has an obligation to meet the food needs of American citizens.

   C) is based on a free market economy.

   D) uses only entitlement programs to distribute food.

   Answer: C
   Page Ref: 445
   Topic: Conceptual

4) A family of four receives a maximum monthly Food Stamps benefit of

   A) $393.   B) $763.   C) $499.   D) $599.

   Answer: C
   Page Ref: 445
   Topic: Factual

5) The first "food stamp" program was established by Congress in

   A) 1950.   B) 1933.

   C) 1976.   D) none of the above

   Answer: B
   Page Ref: 445
   Topic: Factual

6) The current Food Stamp Act

    A) does not allow noncitizens to be eligible.

    B) is administered by the Department of Health and Human Services.

    C) does not count an applicants home and lot as resources for eligibility purposes.

    D) was passed during the presidency of John F. Kennedy.

Answer: C
Page Ref: 446
Topic: Conceptual

7) Which of the following groups of illegal immigrants are NOT eligible for Food Stamps?

    A) Persons granted conditional entry to the U.S. prior to April 1, 1980.

    B) Persons lawfully admitted for permanent residence with 40 qualifying quarters

    C) Refugees admitted under Section 207

    D) none of the above

Answer: A
Page Ref: 447
Topic: Conceptual

8) In 2003, what percentage of the total U.S. population utilized Food Stamps?

    A) 25   B) 8

    C) 35   D) none of the above

Answer: B
Page Ref: 448
Topic: Factual

9) The WIC program

    A) only provides foodstuffs to those eligible.

    B) is an entitlement program.

    C) is only available to single-parent households.

    D) must rely on Congress to re-authorize funding for its programs.

Answer: D
Page Ref: 449
Topic: Factual

10) In 1985, what percentage of all U.S. farmers filed for bankruptcy?

    A) 1   B) 4   C) 10   D) 6

Answer: B
Page Ref: 455
Topic: Factual

11) The Federal Agricultural Improvement Act

    A) received partisan support in Congress.

    B) replaced traditional subsidies with fixed annual payments.

    C) was a boon to family farms.

    D) saved U.S. tax payers money.

Answer: B
Page Ref: 457
Topic: Factual

12) Which of the following statements about seasonal agricultural laborers is accurate?

    A) Median income for both men and women are about the same.

    B) The use of local social services by laborer families is typically high.

    C) Due to unionization, purchasing power of wages has increased.

    D) One-third of all agricultural laborers owned or were buying a house.

Answer: D
Page Ref: 460
Topic: Factual

13) Which statement is NOT accurate about independent labor contractors in the farm industry?

    A) Contracting grew in reaction to the "Freedom to Farm" program.

    B) Contractors shield large growers from legal claims.

    C) Contractors offer few benefits.

    D) Contractors have a history of abusing laborers.

Answer: A
Page Ref: 460
Topic: Applied

14) Which of the following statements is NOT accurate about corporate farming?

    A) They receive a disproportionate amount of subsidy relative to numbers of family farms.

    B) Typically, these farms own all aspects of production.

    C) They are highly specialized operations.

    D) It is consistent with the principle of maintaining open, competitive markets.

Answer: D
Page Ref: 462
Topic: Conceptual

15) The term "sustainable development" refers to

    A) meeting the environmental needs of future generations.

    B) thinking globally about resource issues.

    C) finding a balance between development and open space.

    D) all of the above

Answer: A
Page Ref: 464
Topic: Conceptual

16) Less than 30 percent of laborer housing in eight major agricultural states lacked inside running water.

Answer: FALSE
Page Ref: 460
Topic: Factual

17) Expenditures for the U.S. Department of Agriculture food assistance programs totaled about $46.6 billion in 2004.

Answer: TRUE
Page Ref: 434
Topic: Factual

18) Women and children made up 28 percent of the food insecure population.

Answer: FALSE
Page Ref: 443
Topic: Factual

19) USDA data show that only 45 percent of households with incomes below the poverty line have an adequate level of basic nutrition.

Answer: FALSE
Page Ref: 443
Topic: Factual

20) The single common factor connecting diverse groups of individuals to the problem of hunger is poverty.

Answer: TRUE
Page Ref: 443
Topic: Conceptual

21) More than half of families with children seeking emergency food assistance are single–parent households.

Answer: TRUE
Page Ref: 444
Topic: Conceptual

22) Eighty five percent of the nation's hungry were between the ages of 18 and 65.

Answer: TRUE
Page Ref: 444
Topic: Factual

23) Receiving Food Stamps increases the nutritional value of a low-income household's home food supplies by 20 to 40 percent

Answer: TRUE
Page Ref: 445
Topic: Factual

24) The gross monthly income for a family of 4 at 130% of the poverty line was $2,043.

Answer: TRUE
Page Ref: 448
Topic: Factual

25) A family of any size qualifies for WIC if their household income is below $16,613 per year.

Answer: TRUE
Page Ref: 449
Topic: Factual

26) What are some of the problems associated with undernourished children? Are there economic impacts?

Answer: A detailed discussion of the ramifications of undernourished American children is found on page 444.
Page Ref: 444
Topic: Conceptual

27) What can cause food insecurity?

Answer: Job loss, gaining a household member, or losing food stamps places stress on a household budget. Many households must choose between providing for their food needs and paying rent, bills, etc.
Page Ref: 444
Topic: Applied

28) What percentage of eligible persons receive Food Stamps? Why do you think this number is so low?

Answer: It is estimated that only 50% of those eligible actually receive the Food Stamp benefit. Student answers as to why this number is so low will vary.
Page Ref: 447
Topic: Conceptual

29) What are the work requirements for Food Stamp eligibility?

Answer: Able–bodied adults between 16 & 60 must register for work, accept suitable employment, and take part in an employment and training program, to which they are referred by the food stamp office.

Page Ref: 447
Topic: Conceptual

30) What are the twin goals of WIC?

Answer: The twin goals are to enrich the food intake of participants by providing them food or with coupons to purchase food and to educate mothers, individually and in groups, regarding how to prevent nutritional difficulties.

Page Ref: 448
Topic: Applied

31) What are the six categories of participants in the WIC program?

Answer: The categories include: infants from 0–3 months; infants from 4–12 months; women and children with special dietary needs; children from one to five years; pregnant and nursing mothers; and postpartum nursing mothers.

Page Ref: 448
Topic: Conceptual

32) How, and with what, has the federal government responded to the issue of hunger in the U.S.?

Answer: The Federal Government has many programs designed to combat hunger, including: food stamps, commodity distribution programs, the nation school lunch and breakfast programs, the Special Milk Program, the Special Supplemental Nutrition Program for Women, Infants, and Children (WIC), the Child and Adult Care Food Program, the Summer Food Service Program, Meals on Wheels, and the Congregate Dining Program.

Page Ref: 450
Topic: Applied

33) In your opinion, have the Food Programs worked? Why or why not?

Answer: Student answers to this question will vary.
Page Ref: 451
Topic: Applied

34) What is the School Breakfast Program (SBP)?

Answer: The SBP provides breakfasts to some 8.2 million children in more than 78,000 schools and institutions. It seeks to provide breakfast to promote learning readiness and health eating behavior. Breakfasts served as a part of the SBP provide one-fourth or more of the RDA levels set forth by the federal government.

Page Ref: 452
Topic: Conceptual

35) Cite at least three examples of food stamp bureaucracy.

Answer: More than half of states have food stamp applications that are 10–36 pages long, they are often difficult to read and complete, and they include excessive and invasive questions, often with little or no legal connection to the FS program.
Page Ref: 454
Topic: Conceptual

36) What are the pros and cons of government subsidies to farmers?

Answer: Answers to this question will vary based on student opinions.
Page Ref: 456
Topic: Applied

37) What were the three distinctions of the Food Security Act of 1985?

Answer: It was the most complicated farm bill ever passed, it cost the federal government more than previous farm bills (about $80 billion from 1986–1990) and the price supports, in terms of parity, were lower than they had been in previous legislation.
Page Ref: 456
Topic: Conceptual

38) Why is the profession of farming declining?

Answer: According to the authors, several factors influence the decline in U.S. farming practice, including shrinking farms, lower farming incomes, aging farmer population, consolidation of land and farming practice, a drop in crop prices, lack of efficiency in farming practice.
Page Ref: 457
Topic: Conceptual

39) Give a brief overview of the demographics of U.S. farmworkers.

Answer: Information included on page 459 discusses in great detail the demographic makeup and other characteristics of the U.S. farm working population.
Page Ref: 459
Topic: Applied

40) Discuss at least three of the current issues facing farmers and the profession of farming.

Answer: Genetic engineering, global trade, Mad Cow disease, local selling, organic farming, sustainable agriculture issues, global warming and the economy are mentioned, among others, as being current, serious issues facing farmers in the United States.
Page Ref: 463
Topic: Applied

Chapter 18 The American Welfare State in International Perspective

1) What incident caused the Three World formulation to lose utility?

   A) the formation of OPEC

   B) the introduction of capitalism to China, North Korea and Cuba

   C) fall of the Berlin Wall

   D) the Cold War

   Answer: C
   Page Ref: 472
   Topic: Conceptual

2) Institutional welfare refers to

   A) provision of services in institutions.

   B) provision of services in an inpatient psychiatric center.

   C) provision of services in a bureaucratic style.

   D) provision of services to the population as a whole.

   Answer: C
   Page Ref: 472
   Topic: Conceptual

3) The three-part classification of nations is based on

   A) type of social welfare system.   B) type of government.

   C) age of government.   D) none of the above.

   Answer: B
   Page Ref: 472
   Topic: Factual

4) Residual welfare refers to

   A) serving the poor.

   B) serving the whole population.

   C) utilizing budget surplus to provide social services.

   D) serving residual citizens.

   Answer: A
   Page Ref: 472
   Topic: Conceptual

5) The Four Tigers are

    A) the four most heavily populated nations in the world.

    B) Asian nations with a well-developed military.

    C) Asian nations with more aggressive governments.

    D) Asian nations with high levels of growth.

Answer: D
Page Ref: 472
Topic: Factual

6) Whatpercentof GDP does the U.S. expend for public benefits?

    A) 37.6   B) 24.4   C) 17.1   D) 49.8

Answer: C
Page Ref: 474
Topic: Factual

7) What is pointed to as being the primary incident that created the "underclass?"

    A) World War I   B) the fall of communism

    C) Reductions in welfare benefits   D) all of the above

Answer: C
Page Ref: 476
Topic: Factual

8) The Gini coeffecient is used to gauge national development in what areas?

    A) environmental quality   B) educational level

    C) income   D) all of the above

Answer: C
Page Ref: 476
Topic: Factual

9) The Weighted Index of Social Progress

    A) focuses on health and education issues.

    B) focuses on economic and political factors.

    C) is based on diversity.

    D) all of the above

Answer: D
Page Ref: 477
Topic: Factual

10) Estes' Weighted Index of Social Progress ranks social progress based on how many variables?

    A) 46   B) 10   C) 2   D) 37

Answer: A
Page Ref: 477
Topic: Factual

11) The Human Development Index considers which of the following variables when determining the rank of the development of nations?

  A) life expectancy
  B) income
  C) educational attainment
  D) all of the above

Answer: D
Page Ref: 477
Topic: Factual

12) The U.S. ranks _____ on the WISP; the UK ranks _____ on the same index.

  A) 33; 165
  B) 3; 11
  C) 27;11
  D) 11; 27

Answer: C
Page Ref: 478
Topic: Factual

13) Which of the following is consistently ranked in the top 5 of nations, regardless of the measurement used?

  A) Sweden
  B) United States
  C) Japan
  D) Norway

Answer: A
Page Ref: 478
Topic: Factual

14) Who developed the philosophical rationale for capability poverty?

  A) Martha Nussbaum
  B) Emily Maxwell
  C) Amartya Sen
  D) Richard Estes

Answer: C
Page Ref: 484
Topic: Factual

15) What percentage of South Asian residents live on $1 or less per day?

  A) 40
  B) 60
  C) 20
  D) 10

Answer: A
Page Ref: 488
Topic: Factual

16) Harold Wilensky and Charles Lebeaux assert that social policy in the United States is essentially residualist in nature.

Answer: TRUE
Page Ref: 472
Topic: Factual

17) Social welfare policy in many European nations is residualist in nature.

Answer: FALSE
Page Ref: 472
Topic: Factual

18) The approach to welfare status involving efforts of some countries to forge strong alliances among government, labor, and business in order to reach a consensus on social welfare issues is known as corporatism.

Answer: TRUE
Page Ref: 473
Topic: Factual

19) Since the early 1970s, most Western governments have increased spending or promoted the growth of welfare programs.

Answer: FALSE
Page Ref: 475
Topic: Factual

20) Western industrialized nations pursued liberal social policies after World War II.

Answer: FALSE
Page Ref: 475
Topic: Factual

21) According to Jeffery Sachs, the U.S. will spend similar amounts on defense and official development assistance.

Answer: FALSE
Page Ref: 477
Topic: Conceptual

22) Martha Nussbaum asserts that the most chronically oppressed among the world's poor are women.

Answer: TRUE
Page Ref: 485
Topic: Factual

23) The traditional means of dispersing international aid has been through intergovernmental transfers of money.

Answer: TRUE
Page Ref: 486
Topic: Factual

24) The U.S. has been consistently ranked among the top three of nations providing international aid in relation to their GDP.

Answer: FALSE
Page Ref: 486
Topic: Applied

25) The Bretton Woods agreement established the International Monetary Fund.

Answer: FALSE
Page Ref: 486
Topic: Factual

26) How does the U.S. compare with other nations in regard to its welfare state? Explain your answer using examples from class and the text.

Answer: This question will provide the instructor with the ability to ascertain students' grasp of the chapter material. Answers will vary.
Page Ref: 472
Topic: Applied

27) Explain the three-part classification employed to depict the comparative levels of development of nations.

Answer: The three-part classification includes a First World (Western industrialized nations); a Second World (communist nations that constructed political economies as an alternative to the market-dominated First World); and the Third World (former colonies of the First World, often achieving liberation through revolution).
Page Ref: 472
Topic: Factual

28) What does the phrase "Fourth World" imply?

Answer: This depicts an emerging status of nations that have, over the years, become less developed than they were after receiving independence from a First World nation. These countries have poor infrastructure and unstable political regimes.
Page Ref: 472
Topic: Conceptual

29) Discuss the different typologies used when describing the welfare state.

Answer: Students should point out the various typologies used to describe the welfare state. Different explanations exist, but students should show that they recognize the differences between residual and institutional welfare, corporatist and noncorporatist, liberal welfare state and social democratic welfare state, democratic welfare state, social market welfare state, corporate market welfare state, and the liberal collectivist welfare state. Although these typologies differ, they use similar criteria when classifying countries, primarily including whether or not government social programs exist.
Page Ref: 472
Topic: Conceptual

30) Contrast the ideology behind residual and institutional welfare.

Answer: Residual welfare refers to providing a minimal safety net for the poorest sections of the population rather than catering for the population as a whole. The institutional approach seeks to provide a variety of social programs for the whole population and to combine economic and social objectives in an effort to enhance the well-being of all.
Page Ref: 472
Topic: Applied

31) Discuss at least two theories behind the US' "welfare exceptionalism."

Answer: Theories behind why the U.S. is considered to be unwilling to emphasize government social welfare programs can be found on page 473 & 474.
Page Ref: 473
Topic: Conceptual

32) Some contend that the notion of American welfare state exceptionalism is an unfair criticism. What reasons are given?

Answer: Students should be able to list reasons why the welfare state in America is often unfairly criticized. The most profound argument in this area is the "apples and oranges" argument, meaning that it is impossible to compare the U.S. to other smaller, economically different countries that offer more federally subsidized social welfare programs.
Page Ref: 474
Topic: Applied

33) What do welfare pluralists assert regarding unfavorable comparisons between the U.S. and other countries?

Answer: WP claim that unfavorable comparisons between the U.S. and other countries are based on the idea that state involvement in social welfare is a good thing. They reject his assertion and do not believe that social needs should be met primarily by the government. Instead of relying only on the states for social welfare, welfare pluralists argue that people can enhance their well-being through their own efforts.
Page Ref: 475
Topic: Conceptual

34) Discuss at least 3 of the 5 tenets called for in the 1980s by conservatives regarding welfare reform.

Answer: These concepts called for making welfare benefits contingent on employment, transform open-ended entitlements to discretionary programs; containing the growth of the governmental sector and retain programs that affect the elderly and working poor; replacing government with other institutions; contracting out services and benefits to the private sector.
Page Ref: 476
Topic: Conceptual

35) Agree or disagree with this statement and provide support for your decision: "Solidarity , social citizenship, the gift relationship,and the difference principle — all of them representing formulations of the idea that who live in a society are obligated to insure the welfare of everyone else — are terms bandied about in academic circles, but they no longer make much of an appearance in real politics."

Answer: Students' answers to this conceptual question will vary.
Page Ref: 476
Topic: Conceptual

36) Contrast the Gini coeffecient with the weighted index of social progress. Which is more valid?

Answer: Because the Gini coeffecient only measures income, many social scientist believe the weighted index is more valid because it looks at nations according to their performance in 46 variables, grouped into 10 sub-indices, including: education, health, defense, economic factors, political participation, welfare, cultural diversity, women, demography, geography.

Page Ref: 477
Topic: Conceptual

37) Explain the concept of capability poverty.

Answer: This concept essentially describes freedom is a pre-condition of development, not a development. Those who are in countries with dictatorships, lack of freedom, etc. are more likely to be capable of poverty.

Page Ref: 484
Topic: Applied

38) Explain the two entities that have facilitated growth in the 3rd World since the 1960s.

Answer: These two organizations, which students should be able to describe, include the General Agreement on Tariffs and Trade (GATT) and World Trade Organization (WTO).

Page Ref: 487
Topic: Factual

39) Name the three NGO's that have become well established or show promised of breaking ground in development circles.

Answer: These three NGO's are: Habitat for Humanity, the Grameen Development Bank, and First Nations Development Institute.

Page Ref: 489
Topic: Factual

40) Explain how and why the First Nations Development Institute regards welfare & poverty.

Answer: Though started initially to end the dependence of Nation Americans on the federal government, the FNDI now exists to serve all indigenous peoples. The entity's approach includes a look at: community, nature, subsistence, and nature, as being antithetical to to the model of the industrial West.

Page Ref: 490
Topic: Applied

Teaching Tips for First-time Instructors and Adjunct Professors

Teaching Tips Contents

1 How to be an Effective Teacher

(Adapted from Royse, *Teaching Tips for College and University Instructors: A Practical Guide*, published by Allyn & Bacon, Boston, MA, ©2001, by Pearson Education)

A look at 50 years of research "on the way teachers teach and learners learn" reveals seven broad principles of good teaching practice (Chickering and Gamson, 1987).

1. Frequent student-faculty contact: Faculty who are concerned about their students and their progress and who are perceived to be easy to talk to, serve to motivate and keep students involved. Things you can do to apply this principle:
- ✓ Attend events sponsored by students.
- ✓ Serve as a mentor or advisor to students.
- ✓ Keep "open" or "drop-in" office hours.

2. The encouragement of cooperation among students: There is a wealth of research indicating that students benefit from the use of small group and peer learning instructional approaches. Things you can do to apply this principle:
- ✓ Have students share in class their interests and backgrounds.
- ✓ Create small groups to work on projects together.
- ✓ Encourage students to study together.

3. Active learning techniques: Students don't learn much by sitting in the classroom listening; they must talk about what they are learning, write about it, relate to it, and apply it to their lives. Things you can do to apply this principle:
- ✓ Give students actual problems or situations to analyze.
- ✓ Use role-playing, simulations or hands-on experiments.
- ✓ Encourage students to challenge ideas brought into class.

4. Prompt feedback: Learning theory research has consistently shown that the quicker the feedback, the greater the learning. Things you can do to apply this principle:
- ✓ Return quizzes and exams by the next class meeting.
- ✓ Return homework within one week.
- ✓ Provide students with detailed comments on their written papers.

5. Emphasize time on task: This principle refers to the amount of actual involvement with the material being studied and applies, obviously, to the way the instructor uses classroom instructional time. Faculty need good time-management skills. Things you can do to apply this principle:
- ✓ Require students who miss classes to make up lost work.
- ✓ Require students to rehearse before making oral presentations.
- ✓ Don't let class breaks stretch out too long.

6. Communicating high expectations: The key here is not to make the course impossibly difficult, but to have goals that can be attained as long as individual learners stretch and work hard, going beyond what they already know. Things you can do to apply this principle:
- ✓ Communicate your expectations orally and in writing at the beginning of the course.
- ✓ Explain the penalties for students who turn work in late.
- ✓ Identify excellent work by students; display exemplars if possible.

7. Respecting diverse talents and ways of learning: Within any classroom there will be students who have latent talents and some with skills and abilities far beyond any that you might imagine. Understanding your students as individuals and showing regard for their unique talents is "likely to facilitate student growth and development in every sphere – academic, social, personal, and vocational" (Sorcinelli, 1991, p.21). Things you can do to apply this principle:

- ✓ Use diverse teaching approaches.
- ✓ Allow students some choice of readings and assignments.
- ✓ Try to find out students' backgrounds and interests.

 Tips for Thriving: Creating an Inclusive Classroom

How do you model an open, accepting attitude within your classroom where students will feel it is safe to engage in give-and-take discussions? Firstly, view students as individuals instead of representatives of separate and distinct groups. Cultivate a climate that is respectful of diverse viewpoints, and don't allow ridicule, defamatory or hurtful remarks. Try to encourage everyone in the class to participate, and be alert to showing favoritism.

---

2   Today's Undergraduate Students

(Adapted from: Lyons et al, *The Adjunct Professor's Guide to Success*, published by Allyn & Bacon, Boston, MA, ©1999, by Pearson Education)

Total enrollment in all forms of higher education has increased over 65% in the last thirty years. Much of this increase was among part-time students who now comprise over 70% of total college enrollment. The number of "nontraditional" students, typically defined as 25 years of age or older, has been growing more rapidly than the number of "traditional" students, those under 25 years of age. Though there is a great deal of common ground between students of any age, there are some key differences between younger and older students.

Traditional students: Much more than in previous generations, traditional students are the products of dysfunctional families and have had a less effective primary and secondary education. Traditional students have been conditioned by the aftermath of high-profile ethical scandals (such as Watergate), creating a mindset of cynicism and lack of respect for authority figures – including college professors. Students of this generation are quick to proclaim their "rights". Many of today's students perceive professors as service providers, class attendance as a matter of individual choice, and grades as "pay" to which they are entitled for meeting standards they perceive as reasonable.

Nontraditional students: Many older students are attending college after a long lay-off, frequently doubting their ability to succeed. The other time-consuming challenges in their lives – children, work, caring for aging parents – often prevent adequate preparation for class or contribute to frequent absences. While traditional students demand their "rights," many older students won't ask for the smallest extra consideration (e.g., to turn a project in a few days late). Most older students learn best by doing, by applying the theory of the textbook to the rich set of experiences they have accumulated over the years.

Emerging influences: Today, a fourth of all undergraduate students are members of minority groups. Obviously, ethnicity, language, religion, culture, and sexual orientation are each significant issues to which a professor should be sensitive. The successful professor sees these differences as an opportunity rather than a threat to learning.

 Tips for Thriving: Be a "Facilitator of Learning"

Be energized by students who "don't get it" rather than judgmental of their shortcomings. View yourself as a "facilitator of learning" rather than a "sage on a stage."

What students want from college professors: While each student subgroup has particular characteristics that affect the dynamics of a college learning environment, students consistently need the following from their college instructors:

✓ Consistently communicated expectations of student performance that are reasonable in quantity and quality
✓ Sensitivity to the diverse demands on students and reasonable flexibility in accommodating them
✓ Effective use of classroom time
✓ A classroom environment that includes humor and spontaneity
✓ Examinations that address issues properly covered in class and are appropriate to the level of the majority of the students in the class
✓ Consistently positive treatment of individual students

The new paradigm of "colleges and universities as service providers to consumer-oriented students" is now firmly entrenched. The successful professor will do well to embrace it.

3   Planning Your Course

(Adapted from Royse, *Teaching Tips for College and University Instructors: A Practical Guide*, published by Allyn & Bacon, Boston, MA, ©2001, by Pearson Education)

Constructing the syllabus: The syllabus should clearly communicate course objectives, assignments, required readings, and grading policies. Think of the syllabus as a stand-alone document. Those students who miss the first or second meeting of a class should be able to learn most of what they need to know about the requirements of the course from reading the syllabus. Start by collecting syllabi from colleagues who have recently taught the course you will be teaching and look for common threads and themes.

Problems to avoid: One mistake commonly made by educators teaching a course for the first time is that they may have rich and intricate visions of how they want students to demonstrate comprehension and synthesis of the material, but they somehow fail to convey this information to those enrolled. Check your syllabus to make sure your expectations have been fully articulated. Be very specific. Avoid vaguely worded instructions:

Instruction	Students may interpret as:
"Write a short paper."	Write a paragraph.
	Write half a page.
	Type a two-page paper.
"Keep a log of your experiences."	Make daily entries.
	Make an entry when the spirit moves me.
	At the end of term, record what I recall.
"Obtain an article from the library."	Any magazine article.
	An article from a professional journal.
	A column from a newsletter.

 Tips for Thriving: Visual Quality

Students today are highly visual learners, so you should give special emphasis to the visual quality of the materials you provide to students. Incorporate graphics into your syllabus and other handouts. Color-code your materials so material for different sections of the course are on different colored papers. Such visuals are likely to create a perception among students that you are contemporary.

(Adapted from: Lyons et al, *The Adjunct Professor's Guide to Success*, published by Allyn & Bacon, Boston, MA, ©1999, by Pearson Education)

Success in achieving a great start is almost always directly attributable to the quality and quantity of planning that has been invested by the course professor. If the first meeting of your class is to be successful, you should strive to achieve seven distinct goals.

Create a Positive First Impression: Renowned communications consultant Roger Ailes (1996) claims you have fewer than 10 seconds to create a positive image of yourself. Students are greatly influenced by the visual component; therefore you must look the part of the professional professor. Dress as you would for a professional job interview. Greet each student entering the room. Be approachable and genuine.

Introduce Yourself Effectively: Communicate to students who you are and why you are credible as the teacher of the course. Seek to establish your approachability by "building common ground," such as stating your understanding of students' hectic lifestyles or their common preconceptions toward the subject matter.

Clarify the Goals and Expectations: Make an acetate transparency of each page of the syllabus for display on an overhead projector and using a cover sheet, expose each section as you explain it. Provide clarification and elicit questions.

Conduct an Activity that Introduces Students to Each Other: Students' chances of being able to complete a course effectively is enhanced if each comes to perceive the classmates as a "support network." The small amount of time you invest in an icebreaker will help create a positive classroom atmosphere and pay additional dividends throughout the term.

 Tips for Thriving: Icebreaker

The following activity allows students to get acquainted, exchange opinions, and consider new ideas, values or solutions to problems. It's a great way to promote self-disclosure or an active exchange of viewpoints.

Procedure

1. Give students one or more Post-it™ notes
2. Ask them to write on their note(s) one of the following:
   a. A *value* they hold
   b. An *experience* they have had recently
   c. A *creative idea* or solution to a problem you have posed
   d. A *question* they have about the subject matter of the class
   e. An *opinion* they hold about a topic of your choosing
   f. A *fact* about themselves or the subject matter of the class
3. Ask students to stick the note(s) on their clothing and circulate around the room reading each other's notes.
4. Next, have students mingle once again and negotiate a trade of Post-it™ notes with one another. The trade should be based on a desire to possess a particular value, experience, idea, question, opinion or fact for a short period of time. Set the rule that all trades have to be two-way. Encourage students to make as many trades as they like.
5. Reconvene the class and ask students to share what trades they made and why. (e.g., "I traded for a note that Sally had stating that she has traveled to Eastern Europe. I would really like to travel there because I have ancestors from Hungary and the Ukraine.")

(Adapted from: Silverman, *Active Learning: 101 Strategies to Teach Any Subject*, published by Allyn & Bacon, Boston, MA, ©1996, by Pearson Education).

Learn Students' Names: A student who is regularly addressed by name feels more valued, is invested more effectively in classroom discussion, and will approach the professor with questions and concerns.

Whet Students' Appetite for the Course Material: The textbook adopted for the course is critical to your success. Your first meeting should include a review of its approach, features, and sequencing. Explain to students what percentage of class tests will be derived from material from the textbook.

Reassure Students of the Value of the Course: At the close of your first meeting reassure students that the course will be a valuable learning experience and a wise investment of their time. Review the reasons why the course is a good investment: important and relevant content, interesting classmates, and a dynamic classroom environment.

5   Strategies for Teaching and Learning

(Adapted from: Silverman, *Active Learning: 101 Strategies to Teach Any Subject,* published by Allyn & Bacon, Boston, MA, ©1996, by Pearson Education)

Getting participation through active learning: To learn something well, it helps to hear it, see it, ask questions about it, and discuss it with others. What makes learning "active"? When learning is active, students do most of the work: they use their brains to study ideas, solve problems, and apply what they learn. Active learning is fast-paced, fun, supportive, and personally engaging. Active learning cannot occur without student participation, so there are various ways to structure discussion and obtain responses from students at any time during a class. Here are ten methods to get participation at any time:

1. **Open discussion**. Ask a question and open it up to the entire class without further structuring.
2. **Response cards**. Pass out index cards and request anonymous answers to your questions.
3. **Polling**. Design a short survey that is filled out and tallied on the spot.
4. **Subgroup discussion**. Break students into subgroups of three or more to share and record information.
5. **Learning partners**. Have students work on tasks with the student sitting next to them.
6. **Whips**. Go around the group and obtain short responses to key questions – invite students to pass if they wish.
7. **Panels**. Invite a small number of students to present their views in front of the class.
8. **Fishbowl**. Ask a portion of the class to form a discussion circle and have the remaining students form a listening circle around them. Bring new groups into the inner circle to continue the discussion.
9. **Games**. Use a fun exercise or quiz game to elicit students' ideas, knowledge, or skill.
10. **Calling on the next speaker**. Ask students to raise their hands when they want to share their views and ask the current speaker to choose the next speaker.

(Adapted from Royse, *Teaching Tips for College and University Instructors: A Practical Guide*, published by Allyn & Bacon, Boston, MA, ©2001, by Pearson Education)

Team learning: The essential features of this small group learning approach, developed originally for use in large college classrooms are (1) relatively permanent heterogeneous task groups; (2) grading based on a combination of individual performance, group performance, and peer evaluation; (3) organization of the course so that the majority of class time is spent on small group activities; (4) a six-step instructional process similar to the following model:

1. Individual study of material outside of the class is assigned.
2. Individual testing is used (multiple choice questions over homework at the beginning of class)
3. Groups discuss their answers and then are given a group test of the same items. They then get immediate feedback (answers).
4. Groups may prepare written appeals of items.

5. Feedback is given from instructor.
6. An application-oriented activity is assigned (e.g. a problem to be solved requiring input from all group members).

If you plan to use team learning in your class, inform students at the beginning of the course of your intentions to do so and explain the benefits of small group learning. Foster group cohesion by sitting groups together and letting them choose "identities" such as a team name or slogan. You will need to structure and supervise the groups and ensure that the projects build on newly acquired learning. Make the projects realistic and interesting and ensure that they are adequately structured so that each member's contribution is 25 percent. Students should be given criteria by which they can assess and evaluate the contributions of their peers on a project-by-project basis (Michaelsen, 1994).

 Tips for Thriving: Active Learning and Lecturing

Lecturing is one of the most time-honored teaching methods, but does it have a place in an active learning environment? There are times when lecturing can be effective. Think about the following when planning a lecture:

Build Interest: Capture your students' attention by leading off with an anecdote or cartoon.
Maximize Understanding and Retention: Use brief handouts and demonstrations as a visual backup to enable your students to see as well as hear.
Involve Students during the Lecture: Interrupt the lecture occasionally to challenge students to answer spot quiz questions.
Reinforce the Lecture: Give students a self-scoring review test at the end of the lecture.

6   Grading and Assessment Techniques

(Adapted from Wankat, *The Effective, Efficient Professor: Teaching, Scholarship and Service*, published by Allyn & Bacon, Boston, MA, ©2002, by Pearson Education)

Philosophy of grading: Develop your own philosophy of grading by picturing in your mind the performance of typical A students, B students and so on. Try different grading methods until you find one that fits your philosophy and is reasonably fair. Always look closely at students on grade borders – take into account personal factors if the group is small. Be consistent with or slightly more generous than the procedure outlined in your syllabus.

Criterion grading: Professor Philip Wankat writes: "I currently use a form of criterion grading for my sophomore and junior courses. I list the scores in the syllabus that will guarantee the students As, Bs and so forth. For example, a score of 85 to 100 guarantees an A; 75 to 85, a B; 65 to 75, a C; and 55 to 65, a D. If half the class gets above 85% they all get an A. This reduces competition and allows students to work together and help each other. The standard grade gives students something to aim for and tells them exactly what their grade is at any time. For students whose net scores are close to the borders at the end of the course, I look at other factors before deciding a final grade such as attendance."

 Tips for Thriving: Result Feedback

As stated earlier, feedback on results is the most effective of motivating factors. Anxious students are especially hungry for positive feedback. You can quickly and easily provide it by simply writing "Great job!" on the answer sheets or tests. For students who didn't perform well, a brief note such as "I'd love to talk with you at the end of class" can be especially reassuring. The key is to be proactive and maintain high standards, while requiring students to retain ownership of their success.

7 <u>Using Technology</u>

(Adapted from: Sanders, *Creating Learning-Centered Courses for the World Wide Web*, published by Allyn & Bacon, Boston, MA, ©2001, by Pearson Education)

The Web as a source of teaching and learning has generated a great deal of excitement and hyperbole. The Web is neither a panacea nor a demon, but it can be a valuable tool. Among the many misunderstandings about the use of Web pages for teaching and learning is a view that such efforts must encompass an entire course. Like any other tool in a course (e.g. lectures, discussions, films, or field trips) online material can be incorporated to enhance the learning experience.

The best way to start using the Web in a course is with small steps. Developing a single lesson or assignment, a syllabus, or a few well-chosen links makes more sense than trying to develop a whole course without sufficient support or experience. Testing Web materials with a class that regularly meets face-to-face helps a faculty member gauge how well a lesson using the Web works. Making adjustments within the context of a traditional class helps fine-tune Web lessons that may be offered in distance education without face-to-face interaction.

 Tips for Thriving: Using Videos

Generally a videotape should not exceed half and hour in length. Always preview a video before showing it to ensure the content, language, and complexity are appropriate for your students. Include major videos on your syllabus to encourage attendance and integrate them into the context of the course. Plan to evaluate students' retention of the concepts on exams or through reports. Avoid reinforcing the common student perception that watching a video is a time-filler.

By beginning with good practices in learning, we ask not how the new technology can help us do a better job of getting students to learn, but rather we ask how good pedagogy be better implemented with the new technology.

8 <u>Managing Problem Situations</u>

(Adapted from Wankat, *The Effective, Efficient Professor: Teaching, Scholarship and Service*, published by Allyn & Bacon, Boston, MA, ©2002, by Pearson Education)

Cheating: Cheating is one behavior that should not be tolerated. Tolerating cheating tends to make it worse. Prevention of cheating is much more effective than trying to cure it once it has occurred. A professor can prevent cheating by:

- Creating rapport with students
- Gaining a reputation for giving fair tests
- Giving clear instructions and guidelines before, during, and after tests
- Educating students on the ethics of plagiarism
- Requiring periodic progress reports and outlines before a paper is due

Try to develop exams that are perceived as fair and secure by students. Often, the accusation that certain questions were tricky is valid as it relates to ambiguous language and trivial material. Ask your mentor or an experienced instructor to closely review the final draft of your first few exams for these factors.

Tips for Thriving: Discipline

One effective method for dealing with some discipline problems is to ask the class for feedback (Angelo & Cross, 1993) In a one-minute quiz, ask the students, "What can I do to help you learn?" Collate the responses and present them to the class. If behavior such as excessive talking appears in some responses (e.g. "Tell people to shut up") this gives you the backing to ask students to be quiet. Use of properly channeled peer pressure is often effective in controlling undesired behavior

(Adapted from Royse, *Teaching Tips for College and University Instructors: A Practical Guide*, published by Allyn & Bacon, Boston, MA, ©2001, by Pearson Education)

Unmotivated Students: There are numerous reasons why students may not be motivated. The "required course" scenario is a likely explanation – although politics in colonial America is your life's work, it is safe to assume that not everyone will share your enthusiasm. There are also personal reasons such as a death of a loved one or depression. Whenever you detect a pattern that you assume to be due to lack of motivation (e.g. missing classes, not handing assignments in on time, non-participation in class), arrange a time to have the student meet with you outside the classroom. Candidly express your concerns and then listen.

Motivating students is part of the faculty members' job. To increase motivation professors should: show enthusiasm for the topic; use various media and methods to present material; use humor in the classroom; employ activities that encourage active learning; and give frequent, positive feedback.

(Adapted from Baiocco/Waters, *Successful College Teaching*, published by Allyn & Bacon, Boston, MA, ©1998, by Pearson Education)

Credibility Problems. If you are an inexperienced instructor you may have problems with students not taking you seriously. At the first class meeting articulate clear rules of classroom decorum and comport yourself with dignity and respect for students. Try to exude that you are in charge and are the "authority" and avoid trying to pose as the students' friend.

9 Surviving When You're Not Prepared

(Adapted from: Lyons et al, *The Adjunct Professor's Guide to Success*, published by Allyn & Bacon, Boston, MA, ©1999, by Pearson Education)

Despite your thorough course planning, your concern for students, and commitment to the institution, situations will arise – illness, family emergencies – that prevent you from being fully prepared for every class meeting. Most students will excuse one flawed performance during a term, but try to develop contingency plans you can employ on short notice. These might include:

- Recruiting a guest speaker from your circle of colleagues to deliver a presentation that might interest your students.
- Conducting a carousel brainstorming activity, in which a course issue is examined from several perspectives. Divide the students in to groups to identify facts appropriate to each perspective. For example, you might want to do a SWOT analysis (Strengths, Weaknesses, Opportunities, Threats) on a particular organization or public figure.
- Dividing the class into groups of three or four and asking them to develop several questions that would be appropriate for inclusion on your next exam.
- Identify a video at your local rental store that embellishes material from the course.
- Assign students roles (e.g. press, governmental figures, etc.), and conduct a focused analysis of a late-breaking news story related to your course.
- Divide students into groups to work on an assigned course project or upcoming exam.
- As a last resort, admit your inability to prepare a class and allow students input into formulating a strategy for best utilizing class time.

In each case, the key is to shift the initial attention away from yourself (to permit you to gather your thoughts) and onto an activity that engages students in a new and significant way.

10   Improving Your Performance

(Adapted from: Lyons et al, *The Adjunct Professor's Guide to Success*, published by Allyn & Bacon, Boston, MA, ©1999, by Pearson Education)

The instructor who regularly engages in systematic self-evaluation will unquestionably derive greater reward from the formal methods of evaluation commonly employed by colleges and universities. One method for providing structure to an ongoing system of self-evaluation is to keep a journal of reflections on your teaching experiences. Regularly invest 15 or 20 introspective minutes following each class meeting to focus especially on the strategies and events in class that you feel could be improved. Committing your thoughts and emotions enables you to develop more effective habits, build confidence in your teaching performance, and make more effective comparisons later. The following questions will help guide self-assessment:

> *How do I typically begin the class?*
> *Where/How do I position myself in the class?*
> *How do I move in the classroom?*
> *Where are my eyes usually focused?*
> *Do I facilitate students' visual processing of course material?*
> *Do I change the speed, volume, energy, and tone of my voice?*
> *How do I ask questions of students?*
> *How often, and when, do I smile or laugh in class?*
> *How do I react when students are inattentive?*
> *How do I react when students disagree or challenge what I say?*
> *How do I typically end a class?*

 Tips for Thriving: Video-Recording Your Class

In recent years a wide range if professionals have markedly improved their job performance by employing video recorders in their preparation efforts. As an instructor, an effective method might be to ask your mentor or another colleague to tape a 10 to 15 minute mini-lesson then to debrief it using the assessment questions above. Critiquing a videotaped session provides objectivity and is therefore more likely to effect change. Involving a colleague as an informal coach will enable you to gain from their experience and perspective and will reduce the chances of your engaging in self-depreciation.

References

Ailes, R. (1996) *You are the message: Getting what you want by being who you are.* New York: Doubleday.

Chickering, A.W., & Gamson, Z.F. (1987) Seven principles for good practice in undergraduate education. AAHE Bulletin, 39, 3-7.

Michaelson, L.K. (1994). Team Learning: Making a case for the small-group option. In K.W. Prichard & R.M. Sawyer (Eds.), *Handbook of college teaching*. Westport, CT: Greenwood Press.

Sorcinelli, M.D. (1991). Research findings on the seven principles. In A.W. Chickering & Z. Gamson (eds.), *Applying the seven principles of good practice in undergraduate education*. New Directions for Teaching and Learning #47. San Francisco: Jossey-Bass.